Disastrous Preaching

Disastrous Preaching

Preaching in the Aftermath of a Natural Environmental Disaster

JEFF STANFILL

WIPF & STOCK · Eugene, Oregon

DISASTROUS PREACHING
Preaching in the Aftermath of a Natural Environmental Disaster

Copyright © 2022 Jeff Stanfill. All rights reserved. Except for brief quotations in critical publications or reviews, no part of this book may be reproduced in any manner without prior written permission from the publisher. Write: Permissions, Wipf and Stock Publishers, 199 W. 8th Ave., Suite 3, Eugene, OR 97401.

Wipf & Stock
An Imprint of Wipf and Stock Publishers
199 W. 8th Ave., Suite 3
Eugene, OR 97401

www.wipfandstock.com

PAPERBACK ISBN: 978-1-6667-3219-1
HARDCOVER ISBN: 978-1-6667-2559-9
EBOOK ISBN: 978-1-6667-2560-5

02/21/22

All Scripture quotations are from the English Standard Version, © 2001 by Crossway Bibles, a division of Good News Publishers. ESV Text Edition 2011.

To my wife who is the ideal woman with whom to live through a disaster—she can handle it and look good as she does!

And,
To our Lord Jesus Christ and His Church, especially the local one known as
Covenant Community Church.

Give a portion to seven, or even to eight,
for you know not what disaster may happen on earth.

—Ecclesiastes 11:2

Contents

Preface | ix
Acknowledgments | xi
List of Abbreviations | xiii

SECTION ONE
Introduction, Or: "I get to ride on an airboat!" | 1

Chapter One: A True Story | 3
Chapter Two: The Dynamics of One Local Natural Environmental Disaster | 16
Chapter Three: Definitions and Delimitations | 19

SECTION TWO
Toward A Biblical View of Natural Environmental Disasters Or "Everyone talks about the weather, but . . ." | 23

Chapter Four: Noah's Flood | 27
Chapter Five: Joseph's Famine | 32
Chapter Six: Job's Sufferings | 37
Chapter Seven: Joel's Locusts | 46
Chapter Eight: Jerusalem's Famine | 51
Chapter Nine: Further Coaching from Five Biblical Disaster Events | 56

Contents

SECTION THREE
Effects of a Natural Environmental Disaster Upon the Survivors, Or: "Who are these people I'm preaching to?" | 61

Chapter Ten: The Physical | 65
Chapter Eleven: The Psychological | 68
Chapter Twelve: The Sociological | 80
Chapter Thirteen: The Spiritual | 84
Chapter Fourteen: The Community | 87
Chapter Fifteen: The Church | 91
Chapter Sixteen: Further Coaching for Addressing Listener's Needs | 96

SECTION FOUR
Faithful Preaching in a Natural Environmental Disaster, Or: "Preach it!" | 101

Chapter Seventeen: Faithful About the Event | 103
Chapter Eighteen: Faithful Among the Survivors | 107
Chapter Nineteen: Faithful in One's Calling | 114
Chapter Twenty: Faithful to God | 121
Chapter Twenty-One: The Situation Room | 125

Bibliography | 129

Preface

THIS IS A PROJECT I did not want to do. Just as I began my doctoral studies, my family and the congregation I pastor were swept up in a record-making, historic flood. After the encouragement of my doctoral cohort, professors, and the responses of anyone that I spoke with about it, I decided to do the necessary work to redeem potential good from what happened.

After one's community has experienced an earthquake, a wildfire, a tsunami, a hurricane, a tornado outbreak, or any other natural environmental disaster, there are differences and challenges to preaching that were not present the Sunday before. This book is intended to orient preachers to those differences and challenges, to give a preacher the basic biblical building blocks to develop one's own scriptural view of the event and all that follows a disaster, and to provide coaching for preaching in the aftermath of a natural environmental disaster.

The brief inclusion of my personal story and details of other pastors' stories is for two reasons. The first is to give the reader an idea that I write from some degree of personal experience, though I do realize that my experience is neither universal nor exhaustive. The second reason is my main motivation—to simply celebrate God! In our story—as in the story of every one of his children—God is faithful! I want to write that again—God is faithful!

It is crucial for the reader to also know that the guidance given in what follows is not only from my experience. What is written here is distilled from academic qualitative research among other local pastors who ministered during the Baton Rouge Flood of 2016.

Preface

While the observations are drawn from a specific event, I believe that what is passed along here is universally applicable within usual human limits.

Like grief, experiencing any natural environmental disaster has common elements. Many people experience the loss of a spouse, parents, a child, a friend. But the loss of *that* spouse, *that* parent, *that* child, and *that* friend by *this* person is unique. In that way the impact of a natural environmental disaster will be navigated somewhat uniquely by a locale, a church, a pastor, or an individual. But much can still be learned from the common experience.

The book is arranged into four sections, each of which addresses a different area of fundamental knowledge that is helpful for a preacher in a natural environmental disaster. The chapters in each section are as brief as possible while still providing helpful content. Many chapters conclude with offering coaching for your preaching relative to their topics. Sections Two and Three each conclude with a full chapter that offers further coaching for preaching that is drawn from the considerations given within their chapters. Hopefully, this arrangement will help you if you are actively preaching in a disaster's aftermath.

This book is intentionally concise. While it is written for both the academy and the local pastor, it favors the local pastor who is in the midst of a natural environmental disaster. Ideally you will have read this book before any event has occurred. But it is also possible that you are reading this while living in the rescue, recovery, and rebuilding that follows a disaster. In that case, you quickly need to know what you need to know. Hence the concise nature of this book.

If you are reading this having survived a natural environmental disaster yourself, your story plot will have different twists, turns, and the unexpected. But I am convinced that something we both will share is this—God is faithful!

> ". . . *that people may know from the rising of the sun and from the west that there is none besides me; I am the Lord and there is no other. I form light and create darkness: I make well-being and create calamity:*
> *I am the Lord, who does all these things."*
> Isaiah 45:6–7

Acknowledgments

I AM GRATEFUL FOR the encouragement and mentoring of my dissertation supervisor, Dr. Calvin Pearson. He was the first to plant and then water the idea of my writing this book. Among others who encouraged with their kind reading and honest but helpful critiquing of the manuscript are Jim Gilliam (my best friend for over thirty-five years now) and Bryan Stell (whose talents as cartoonist, humorist, teacher, leader, pastor, and all-around good guy are highly admirable). And Alex Stanfill gets a big shout-out for doing some heavy lifting in getting the manuscript into good form and offering his insights. Thanks, son.

There is a wonderful group of people known as Covenant Community Church that I want to acknowledge for their love for Christ, their character, and perseverance. My wife and I have been honored to fill the role of pastor to them for over two decades now. God has used them to help me grow and develop into more of who he has called me to be.

There is another special group who cannot be named due to the nature of their calling, their relationships with their parishioners, and their role in the field research for this project. They are fellow colleagues in my pastoral calling, friends within the fraternity called pastors, and respected professionals who in humility serve others and Christ.

You all know who you are! And I want you to know both my deep gratitude for your friendship and my earned respect for each of you.

List of Abbreviations

FEMA   Federal Emergence Management Agency
MHU   Manufactured Housing Unit
NED(S)   Natural Environmental Disaster(s)

SECTION ONE

Introduction,
Or:
"I get to ride on an airboat!"

THIS BOOK IS WRITTEN to help preachers and pastors understand preaching during natural environmental disasters (NEDs). It provides guidance for such preaching. It offers insights gained from personal experience and qualitative research for preachers to be better prepared for a natural disaster and to be more effective as preachers in the aftermath of such an event.

During a natural environmental disaster, there are many dimensions of pastoral and administrative ministry that a pastor is likely called upon to do that is beyond the routine of pastoral work. One may be expected to be a community chaplain available to many more people than just those of his or her own congregation. One may become a relief coordinator, or a shelter supervisor, or an advisor for civic leaders. One's research skills may have to be better honed to glean accurate information to share with parishioners. One may have to gain some medical knowledge if not medical skill to help professionals.

Skills and terms once unknown to a pastor may become second-hand knowledge during the disaster rescue and recovery phases. Typical day-to-day activities and vocabularies of local

SECTION ONE

pastors likely do not include "mucking out"[1] a house, knowing how to hang, tape, and float sheetrock, organizing food distribution, and assessing large-scale financial needs. But very likely these terms, activities, and more will become common place for a pastor during a NED.

In a NED, a pastor is as likely to be a victim as are those to whom one ministers. It is not only the church property nor the families within one's church that need attention and help but one's own family, home, property, and possessions must be cared for, accounted, and secured. Depending upon the nature and extent of the NED the most basic needs for food, water, shelter, and clothing must be procured for one's immediate family while fulfilling one's calling to the congregation and community. As the research from interviews with the pastors in this book project will indicate, preaching during a NED has challenges and rewards not necessarily experienced during the typical week-to-week pulpit ministry.

---

1. "Muck out" is a common, non-technical term used for the work of general cleaning out the debris from flood water, removing damaged material of a building, and often sanitizing the building for preparation for restoration.

CHAPTER ONE

A True Story

The text came mid-Friday morning, August 12th, asking if I had heard that one of our church family's house was flooding. Being surprised by what the text said, I doubted the information. Even a bit of water can easily be exaggerated into a flood. I called the family and immediately knew the text was correct. The sound of the voice over the phone told me the situation was not a bit of water. In a few moments I understood that the family's situation was not going to be addressed simply by helping them gain perspective. Their house was flooding significantly for the first time in the history of the property. The voice on the phone was almost shrill.

I offered to come help and to see if others could be gathered to do the same. I was given assurance that everything that could be done was being done. I gave an offer for them to come to our house if necessary. I committed to stay in touch through the morning.

I did not give any consideration to the possibility that my family's home may flood. As I went to bed that Friday night after nonstop rain, I looked out to check the water in the street. It was over the road up the street but rains like this often did fill that low area of the road surface with water. The next morning it should all be gone.

Awaking a little earlier than usual for a Saturday, I looked out to see that the water level in the street had not changed. That was good because it meant it had at least not risen. Going on with the routines of my morning, I stopped and called the family from the

SECTION ONE

day before. I could not reach them on either home phone or cellphones. I decided that I would later drive over to see them.

A call from a next-door neighbor completely distracted me from later contacting the family from our church. Our neighbor informed my family that the residents in the back of the subdivision—about three quarters of a mile from our house—were flooding and had been instructed to go to the elementary school in our neighborhood for shelter. The alarm was that the water from the Amite River behind our subdivision was less than five blocks from us and coming quickly—prepare for water. Within minutes after the call the water level in the street in front of our house began to rise.

We took necessary precautions, helped our neighbors do the same, and watched as water continued to approach all our houses. Everyone was moving to the school located one block behind our address. We did the same anticipating that perhaps two to three inches of water may get into our house—not the thirty-five inches that did.

Other local pastors were beginning to handle a growing crisis, too. Before sunrise that Saturday, Pastor Clark[1] learned via a Facebook post that two older women of his congregation were unable to leave their homes due to flood water. The Facebook post was from the children of one of the women asking if anyone was able to reach them. The women—sisters—lived side-by-side.

Pastor Clark drove to the flooding subdivision in his SUV. The water was already in their houses when he arrived. Clark helped the women out of their houses and into his vehicle. He drove them to his own house where upon arriving it was discovered that critical medicine had been forgotten back in one of their homes. Ten o'clock that morning Clark headed back to the flooded house, but this time he could not get into the subdivision. He parked his SUV on higher ground at a nearby community college and walked through waist-deep water into the subdivision.

The moment Clark entered the house he saw the refrigerator that stored the medicine topple backwards and began floating in the water. With the refrigerator door being on the topside, he was able

---

1. Other than my name, the names of the pastors have been changed. The stories, however, are as related to me in personal interviews with each.

to retrieve the medicine. It was only later upon reflection that Clark grasped what actually happened. If the refrigerator had toppled on its front, he would not have been able to retrieve the life-sustaining medicine. This was one of many "coincidences" that he would later be able to recount.

No other pastor had quite the weekend as did Pastor Mitchel. He was with forty of his parishioners . . . and twenty of their pets. Families living near the church came to the higher ground on which the church was located as their homes began to flood. But soon the church property and facilities, one of the largest in the city, flooded as well. This included the parsonage. Mitchel and the families were in the upstairs of the church's school with no air conditioning and no lights. Functional plumbing was in another building on the other side of a waist-deep wade through flood water.

For the next three days he and the others waited to be evacuated from the hot and humid building. Cellphone service was spotty. Fortunately, several of the families that retreated into the upstairs of the building had thought to bring some food supplies with them as they fled their flooding homes. The food was shared among everyone as they waited for the water to recede. They whiled away their time chatting, playing card games, and sleeping.

Pastor Brown's experience that Saturday and the months that followed was different than several of his local pastoral friends. The church's parsonage is located a few yards from the church's main building and the church's property fronts a major artery through the city. The four-lane-plus turn-lane road lays atop a roadbed that is several feet higher than all the surrounding properties. This road construction, done many years ago, formed a levee of protection for Brown and his church property. On the other side of the highway from the church most homes, businesses, and properties flooded.

But for Brown there was a different personal challenge the day of the flood which lingered with him for months afterward. So many neighbors, friends, and colleagues flooded. But due to a civil engineering road design, he was spared. Brown self-diagnosed his experience as akin to what is commonly called "survivor's guilt."[2]

---

2. "Survivor's guilt" is a popular term for the stressful aftermath one experiences when not killed as others in a deadly event or, as in this case, not

SECTION ONE

A church of another denomination was located very nearby Brown on the flooding side of the highway. The two are located within sight of one another. As soon as the receding water allowed, the pastor of the other church, Pastor Johnson, got to his church's property to survey what happened. He was confronted with the realization that this was his first experience of this kind. He had no training for such a situation. He did recognize that throughout all their facilities the sheetrock walls had to be cut out from eighteen inches down to the floor.

Pondering this, Johnson considered how the congregation was composed generally of older adults—many of whom were retired. Later he learned that 60% of the homes of families in the church flooded. But the pressing question arose: where could they meet for worship now?

That question began bringing together the stories of Brown and Johnson as Brown's church became an answer for Johnson. Through the local pastors's network in Central, Pastor Brown made an open announcement that their facilities would be made as available as possible to other churches that flooded. First come, first serve. Pastor Johnson arranged with Brown to use their gymnasium for worship on Sunday evenings since the overall facilities were too small for both congregations to meet on the same schedule. Johnson was seeing quickly after the disaster that God provides.

And Brown was realizing more the divine intervention he experienced in the sparing of his family and his congregation's property from the turmoil of flooding. Their location and facilities within days of that weekend became a housing center for relief teams from across the United States. People and churches related to Brown's denomination quickly came with labor, supplies, and finances to help the families of their church who did flood. The teams also helped in the community by mucking out flooded houses for occupants.

Pastor Keith was unable to leave his home the entire weekend of the flood. His house was dry but the streets and roads between him and his church were impassable. The chair of the church

---

affected as severely as others.

trustees who was charged with responsibility for the church facilities could not get to the property either. At the time, Keith was hearing reports of bridges being out. While later it was learned that no bridges had failed, the congregation was still unable to have services that weekend. It would be Monday before he was able to get to the church property.

Once there he was confronted with a flooded office area, choir library, gymnasium, associate pastor's parsonage, and most other facilities. Thankfully, the sanctuary had not received flood water! But his initial sense of shock was in trying to understand what needed to be done to bring everything back.

Like other pastors in the area, he faced the challenge of checking with individuals and families to see how they fared. But this was compounded by the need for identifying volunteers who did not flood to do the immediate stage of work for recovering the church property. While making calls he learned that some of the congregants had been out that weekend rescuing other people from their homes. This was not surprising, as the church had a reputation for being a place where people could come and get the help they needed.

Among the many residences of my neighborhood sheltering at the school the Saturday of the flood was Pastor Roble and his wife. Their home was literally across the street from the school. A few months before the flood, Pastor Roble's wife had been in an injurious car accident. She was recovering from her very painful injuries and the only relief from pain she received in the shelter was to walk non-stop. It was good that the school was less than three-hundred feet from their house. But what was not good was watching the rising waters climb higher and higher on the exterior walls of their home. And if the water was climbing the walls of the exterior, it was climbing the walls of the interior.

By now for me the situation had progressed from feeling adventuresome, to being surreal, to a mixture of feelings of both helplessness and determination at the same time. I was feeling helpless because at the school we were less than two hundred yards from our house. We could watch as the water climbed higher on the sides of our house and there was absolutely nothing we could do about it. Never having been flooded like this, my wife and I had no idea what was ahead.

But the feeling of determination was strong as well. There was a motivation to "work the problem." We talked with the local teacher who was asked by civic officials to manage the school-turned-shelter and volunteered to help him. Doing whatever he needed kept us occupied and allowed me to function with a somewhat professional detachment from the situation. That was helpful for me as I was helpless in doing anything about our house.

Mid-afternoon Saturday, an order came from civil authorities to evacuate the school. Access to the school had become cut off from the rest of the community by the flood water. Evacuation needed to begin immediately to allow time to ferry the hundreds of people out of danger and transport them to another shelter. As boats began to arrive sporadically, the Robles were designated to be among the first taken out due to her injuries. As the Robles approached being next in the queue to board one of the boats, the passenger count indicated the boat was already filled to capacity. Disappointed yet having no choice, they would wait for the next boat.

But what at that moment was a disappointment was actually a divine intervention. While making its circuit to the extraction point, the boat the Robles missed was swamped by the strong, moving water spilling its occupants into the murky river water. All the evacuees aboard the swamped vessel eventually reached safety. But Pastor Roble's wife—if riding in that boat—may not have been able to have been among those reaching safety due to her injuries. The likelihood of further injuries or worse would have been very real for her.

My wife, college-aged son, and I stayed at the school shelter until the next to last boat. This was much later since the first boat ferried evacuees to higher ground. We felt it was our duty to stay since we had volunteered to help the ad hoc shelter director with his responsibilities. And when we did leave is when it happened—I finally got to ride on an airboat! A dream since childhood finally fulfilled but not in any way I had ever thought.

The engine was loud; every inch of the deck of the boat was covered with people or pets. We did not want to move or shift our weight very much to keep the boat stable under its load. And this was not a tour through a Louisiana swamp or a race across the Everglades of Florida. Yet I can still say that I rode on an airboat!

At about 1:00 AM on Sunday, a few miles from our flooded home, my family and I were met by one of our church members in the parking lot of a designated shelter. Thankfully, up to that point cellphone service worked well enough to receive his offer for help. It was an overwhelming sense of relief to see him there waiting for us as we arrived aboard a military high-water transport after evacuating from the school. His familiar and friendly manner gave a moment of reassurance.

The coolness of the air conditioner in his SUV was refreshing. But not nearly as refreshing to eventually settle into a borrowed bed after a hot shower in his family's house. Sunday morning, I learned that we were only one of four other flooded family's staying on his property that night.

The afternoon of the next day, Sunday, our church treasurer and I were able to survey our church property. Thankfully the water had receded quickly in our immediate area. We found that two of the church's three buildings received six to eight inches of water. Nothing could be done that late in the day, so I made phone calls to see who of our congregation could volunteer the next day to help with the initial cleaning out of our flooded buildings. A team of seven men from the church were able to meet me that Monday. Not having flooded themselves they were available at that point in time to begin ripping out flooring, cutting out lower walls, and to unbolt the pews from the floor to prepare for their removal from our building designed to seat over three-hundred and fifty people.

The Monday morning after the flood, civil authorities announced that residents could re-enter our subdivision to check on their properties. As our church treasurer and I rode to the church to begin organizing the volunteers that could come, he spoke frankly and caringly with me as he strongly urged me to go survey my own house and attend to it while they worked on the church that day. It was late that morning, two days after the flood, that my wife and I along with one of our sons walked into our house. We saw firsthand the effects of a river flowing through one's house.

SECTION ONE

The furniture was tossed around. Some was in the wrong rooms. The refrigerator was face down on the kitchen floor. Spots were on the countertops showing that the water had reached that high. The laminate flooring throughout most of the house was flipped over or twisted or shuffled on itself. Our mattresses were soggy sponges. Bookcases were collapsed and volumes of prized books were thoroughly soaked. Mold was already growing inside cabinets throughout the house. Everything that had been in the yard was gone—firewood, patio fixtures, garbage cans. And the automobile we left in the carport, not wanting to risk driving it out in the flooded streets, had been in water up to the side mirrors—and a dead snake dropped out when I opened the door.

We had to have some time to walk through and process what we were surveying. There were no strong emotions as we went from room to room. We would see different features of the destruction and ask odd questions or make strange observations such as "How did the flooring flip around that way?," "Look where this table floated. How did it do that?," and "Why is this chair in this room in the back of the house?" But there would be other days later of plenty of emotions.

The clean-out or mucking out process began immediately. Within the next three days the inventory of our household goods was piled on the edge of the street in front of our house—just like thousands of other residents. One day as I was adding to the pile on the street, I thought how fortunate that who I considered myself to be was not the man that owned this thing or that object. My wife and I were both blessed that God's grace had prevented us from becoming so materialistic that we were vested in our furniture, the labels on our clothing, the age of our appliances, or the "prestige" of our used automobile. Seeing our identity in Christ was a significant blessing for these three days because in the end we salvaged only eight dining room chairs, one sofa table, a coffee table, and the clothes that were able to be cleaned.

During the first week after the flood, like every other week before the flood, preparation needed to be made for preaching that Sunday. And it would be so each week after the flood.

A True Story

The next weekend our first worship service following the natural disaster was surprisingly well attended. People wanted to be together with those they knew well and loved. We were all suffering believers. Over 45% of the families in our church flooded to some extent. The noise level was high that Sunday due to meeting in a space significantly smaller than the sanctuary. More meaningfully, the noise was from the exchanging of stories between friends. Worship understandably began somewhat subdued as emotional reserves were spent by what had happened. As the service continued people became more engaged and aware of the fulfillment of God's promise to be with his people.

I had not coached the worship leader for that day but allowed him to develop the music himself as he usually did. That proved to be good for the congregation as it gave more than my perspective of the day.

An unusual moment occurred in the service as we transitioned from the worship time. Justifiably, soft crying and gentle sobbing could be heard across the crowd. But one person's sobs became louder and grew into a wail. I became very uncomfortable with the moment. If something like this had occurred in a service before that Sunday, I would have gently but clearly asked that it be stopped. But this was not a typical Sunday worship service as it was the gathering of God's people who had just experienced a devastating event corporately as well as individually. I recognized that the loud, sustained, emotional outburst was being a vicarious experience for the congregation. It was as if everyone was allowing their own wailing to be sounded by the one individual. As unique as the moment was, it was also emotionally healthy for the congregation. It was allowed to go on for a short time before continuing with the service plan.

The time came to preach the first sermon after the flood. Being both physically and emotionally exhausted already by the first week following the flood, I honestly could not remember ever feeling weaker in the pulpit. Not even the first time that I preached many years ago had I felt this inadequate or even physically weak. This weakness had been with me during the few hours of sermon preparation amid all the activity of that week. But it came to full bloom

SECTION ONE

in that moment. And as I would for many Sundays for months to come while sharing the Word of God, I genuinely felt the Holy Spirit carrying me through the preaching event. I also sensed the Holy Spirit allowing me to be more aware of the sermon's impact upon the lives of the listeners.

Personally, the next seven months were filled with days of mucking out, learning new procedures for insurance, arranging for a contractor to restore our house, interacting with local, state, and federal officials and bureaucracies, procuring building supplies, searching for replacement furniture, purchasing an automobile, and countless other details. Thankfully, a local friend who had not flooded and was out of town on extended travel offered their house for us to use for several months. Too many families in the community and in our church were squeezed into housing with other family groups for months. Eventually, we ourselves were housed in a manufactured housing unit (MHU) on our own property provided by the Federal Emergency Management Agency (FEMA).

And during those seven months of intense living I, as many other local pastors, prepared and preached sermons each Sunday.

While restoring our house and property I also had the responsibility of the restoration of the church property. Not having flood insurance, the church was exposed to the potential of great loss. The work of the initial team that mucked out our church buildings relieved the pressure to immediately begin restoration of the facilities. Their efforts "froze" the church's building needs for a time. But our financial resources and volunteer potential did not match the task ahead of us.

About nine weeks after the flood, my wife and I had opportunity to be out of town for a week. It was not a vacation for me as each day was filled with meetings. But it was a great change of scenery away from all the damage we saw and lived in every day; it was a welcomed change of pace; it was a welcomed respite. After a week away we felt "normal" again. But I was not expecting what would happen that Sunday morning back at our church.

I arrived at the church early as usual for Sunday. It had been a wonderful week the days before. But when I opened the door to enter our church's main building I stepped back into a partially gutted building of dusty, bare concrete floors with literally one chair and a desk in the entire building. It was as if all the weight of responsibility that had accumulated since August suddenly fell back upon my shoulders not gradually but immediately.

It was an overwhelming experience. And for the first time in my life in any circumstances I had ever been in before, I did not want to do what lay ahead. I felt finished. The determination that motivated me the day of the flood while sheltering in the school was flipped into despondency and overpowering despair. I was not expecting this.

I sat in the one chair in the building and began to cry saying, "God, I do not want to do this. I am through. I can't. And I must preach in about two hours. Father, I cannot!"

In the southern part of the United States, we have a phrase we use for situations like this. It's a "come to Jesus" moment. It can be time to "come to Jesus" for many different reasons but that day for me it was come to Jesus for there was no other place to go or person to whom to turn. Having never felt weaker physically, emotionally, mentally, or spiritually I cried tears directed to Christ.

And in that moment, he graciously and kindly "came to me." In the way that only God can through the work of his Son and the power of his Holy Spirit, he supernaturally strengthened me so that I felt rested again. His energy was renewed within me so that I was motivated again. And his empowering presence became manifest for me. While the work still needed to be done and situations often arose that were challenging, from that moment on God's faithfulness was so recognizable. I was renewed and enabled to preach that day from a posture of victory and faith in Christ.

Personal needs and those of the church were being met all along the way thanks to the financial offerings from across the United States that continued to come to and through our church. As word of the flood spread, responses came from known sources as well as from people and churches previously unknown to our congregation. And just as needed as the money were teams of volunteers from the region. Out of town teams were housed in the upper floor of our church. Temporary showers were installed in our foyer bathrooms for the teams' use. As our congregation was in no position to provide food for the teams, the teams often brought their own food and cooks.

Our church did not want to become inward-focused during the restoration period. From many sources non-perishable foods and supplies were donated to us. In the now empty sanctuary space, we set up one of the several distribution centers for the community. The church also coordinated volunteer teams that made day trips into the area to help people with the initial clean up from the flood waters. This phase of recovery lasted for several months. And each week I, as the other pastors in the area, prepared and preached on Sunday.

To manage the relief and restoration work, I asked three individuals in the church to coordinate and oversee both the relief efforts going out from the church as well as the restoration of the church property. These were people whose homes or businesses did not flood or who were able to get back into their homes quickly. Both general day-to-day activity and lower-level decisions related to the flood were delegated to them. I focused on the major decisions and coordinating help that came to and through us for our community.

Many members of the congregation, whether personally flooded or not, gave time and effort to work at restoring our church building. One set day a week was designated as a workday for any who were available. I was always astonished to see people take a day away from their own restoration work to be there for their church. But the one activity that could not be delegated was preparing and preaching each Sunday.

The restoration process for the church uncovered previously unknown structural issues with our main building. This stalled the last phase of restoration for almost a year. While volunteer teams of varying skill sets and abilities were able with oversight to do much of the other work, this would require professionals. We faced both the lack of funds and know-how. Due to the amount of work being done across the area of Baton Rouge and in our municipality of Central, reputable and local contractors were difficult to obtain. This became a major focus of prayer for our congregation. Eventually reliable bids for the work were received but even the lowest was well beyond our reach.

Again, God's faithfulness was seen! Samaritan's Purse, an international humanitarian agency that specializes in recover and relief efforts, was active in the Baton Rouge area helping residents restore their homes. This has historically been Samaritan's Purse's singular focus in circumstances like this. But seeing the situation of the Baton Rouge flood, the organization made the decision to pilot a program to help churches recover. After several months of prayerfully attempting to collect reliable bids, our church applied for and received a large grant from Samaritan's Purse! The amount enabled the structural issues to be repaired and the restoration work to be completed.

While I was praying for God's provisions to complete the task of restoration, on the one day of the week I was not working on my house, another's house, or the church building, I was praying and preparing to preach each Sunday.

March 25, 2018—nineteen months after the Baton Rouge Flood of 2016—we held a rededication Sunday for the restored buildings! Present that day were the city mayor, Samaritan's Purse representatives, the contractor that repaired the structural issues, and friends who significantly aided the congregation in our great time of need. It was a Sunday of retelling the story of God's faithfulness and celebrating in his presence. And it was the first Sunday in nineteen months that my sermon preparation and preaching was unencumbered by the Baton Rouge Flood of 2016.

CHAPTER TWO

The Dynamics of One Local Natural Environmental Disaster

WHAT HAD HAPPENED THE weekend of August 12–14, 2016? Where did this rain come from? This is South Louisiana which is accustomed to oppressive humidity, high temperatures, heavy rains, and hurricanes. Wind damage and loss of electrical power, managing food and supplies for several days, and doing without modern conveniences during such times is not unusual. But this time was unusual.

First, the amount of rain was record breaking. According to Dr. Josh Eachus, Chief Meteorologist at WBRZ TV, a Baton Rouge affiliate station for the American Broadcast Corporation, an average of twenty inches of rain fell over the four-parish area around Central, Louisiana in two days.[1] Within this area there were reported record-breaking localized rainfall amounts of 31.39 inches, 26.83 inches, and 25.5 inches within a two-day period.[2] Before 2016 the record of rainfall for Louisiana was almost twenty-five inches in Abita Springs in 1995.[3] The Amite River, which flooded over our church and my house, crested at nearly five feet above the previous

---

1. Eachus, interview by author.
2. Advocate staff report, "What Caused the Historic August 2016 Flood..."
3. Advocate staff report, "What Caused the Historic August 2016 Flood..."

The Dynamics of One Local Natural Environmental Disaster

crest record set in 1983.[4] And, the 1983 flood itself had set new records by every metric for the area.

Another significant difference for the Baton Rouge Flood of 2016 was that the geographic expanse of the event meant that an individual's normal support system was as affected as he or she. Past NEDs like hurricanes did not include such large numbers of families and businesses being struck. In 1983, the flood affected 5,471 homes and businesses in the three parishes of Ascension, East Baton Rouge, and Livingston. In 2016, per municipal records, approximately five-thousand one-hundred structures were flooded in Central alone.[5] Other times those who were affected could rely upon extended family members or a neighbor as close as right next door. But this time, someone that flooded could not evacuate to a parent's or sibling's or another relative's house because in all likelihood they had flooded, too.

A third difference for this event was the perceived lack of warning. Local prognosticators began noticing a non-descript area of low pressure in the northeastern Gulf of Mexico on August 7th and 8th.[6] While during annual hurricane season weather observers are attentive to the Gulf of Mexico, a low-pressure system or even a tropical storm near the coast of Louisiana is not going to cause great alarm. Hurricanes are what is on everyone's mind during that time of year.

Wednesday and Thursday before the flood, local broadcast forecasters began sharing with the public the possibility of a slow-moving low-pressure system that could likely bring heavy rains. The possibility of flash-flooding and rising rivers entered the announcements. Over those two days the ground was saturated with several inches of rainwater presenting conditions ripe for flooding from rain.[7] But flash flood warnings are also common during the summer in south Louisiana. Regarding a warning, the public's attention was diverted that week by the news cycle of a significant fire

---

4. Advocate staff report, "What Caused the Historic August 2016 Flood..."
5. Matt Zyjewski, interview by author, Central, Louisiana, January 29, 2018.
6. Eachus, interview by author.
7. Eachus, interview by author.

SECTION ONE

at one of the major industrial plants in the Baton Rouge area. The rains were seen only as an aggravating hinderance in fighting the fire. Local attention was more focused on the plant incident than the weather. The general population apparently was not attuned to what was about to happen.

As the low-pressure system itself moved over the Baton Rouge area it was met by a very weak front from northeast Texas. It was like ". . . closing the door on this storm. There was nowhere for it to go. It was not going to backtrack. It was trying to move west, and it couldn't because of the front."[8] By the weekend of the actual flood, rain amounts were as high as thirty-plus inches in two days with an area average of twenty inches.[9] The consensus among local and state climatologists is that what happened in the Baton Rouge Flood of 2016 was a tropical system that wasn't named as a storm.[10]

As the rains fell across the region of southeastern Louisiana and southwestern Mississippi, the three rivers that flow through the Baton Rouge area began to swell. Two of the rivers—the Comite and the Amite—converge very near Central, LA. The two rivers actual form boundary lines for the city's corporation limits. This compounded the flooding as the run-off through the basin area was too much for the rivers to handle within their banks. Both rivers contributed catastrophically to the situation the Central pastors experienced.

Recovery was different, as well. Initially and ongoing for many months, supplies were limited if not scarce. The percentage of the affected population and properties was exceedingly high which slowed recovery time. Recovery was a marathon not a sprint for the pastors, their congregations, and the thousands of families and businesses around them.

---

8. Advocate staff report, "What Caused the Historic August 2016 Flood . . ."
9. Advocate staff report, "What Caused the Historic August 2016 Flood . . ."
10. Advocate staff report, "What Caused the Historic August 2016 Flood . . ."

CHAPTER THREE
Definitions and Delimitations

WHILE THE WORD *DISASTER* can be used in different ways in different contexts, what is considered disastrous for one individual or group of people may not be seen the same by another. Disaster mental health authors Halpern and Tramontin state that the word disaster "implies sudden misfortune that results in the loss of life or property or in other forms of great harm or damage."[1] In regard to mental health, the very definition of disaster spurs debates and challenges for understanding its effect on survivors.[2] The Humanitarian Disaster Institute of Wheaton College in its guide for disaster chaplaincy avoids defining disasters and instead describes them as ". . . upsetting experiences . . ." before proceeding with insights for equipping one to minister in the aftermath of a disaster.[3]

One understanding of what a disaster is stands out among the others. Disaster research specialist K.J. Tierney defines disasters as ". . . collective stress situations that happen (or at least manifest themselves) relatively suddenly in a particular geographic area, involve some degree of loss, interfere with the ongoing social life of the community, and are subject to human management."[4] It is this

---

1. Halpern and Tramontin, *Disaster Mental Health*, 3.
2. Tierney, *Social and Community Contexts of Disaster*, 12.
3. Aten and Boan, *Spiritual First Aid*, 8.
4. Tierney, *Social and Community Contexts of Disaster*, 12.

definition by which I understand a natural environmental disaster (NED). And, it is this definition with which this book proceeds.

According to psychologist and psychotherapist A.J.W. Taylor, disaster experts categorize disasters in one of three classifications—natural, industrial, or human. The cause of the disaster is the criteria for classification. A human disaster arises from human action whether intentional or unintentional and for any motive.[5] An industrial disaster is one caused by "a serious disruption of the ecosystem from the products, by-products, and waste from the manufacturing system."[6] Taylor cites Whittow's classification of natural disaster as being caused by "profound disruptions of the physical environment" and then charts numerous types of natural disasters ranging from avalanches to tornadoes to floods to droughts and more.[7] Further classification within these three groups is pinpointed according to the elements of the disaster—earth, air, fire, water, or people.[8] These classifications are more than academic for they indicate the way survivors will likely perceive the event, its influence upon them, and more importantly how they react and respond to the event in terms of recovery. This has bearing upon preaching as will be seen later.

As previously noted, disasters occur in many ways. Each can have a unique affect upon a preacher and preaching. One may preach in the context of a financial disaster as did the generation of the 1920s in America during what is called The Great Depression. This is also true of those who have preached more recently in the inflationary crisis such as is commonly reported in Venezuela in the twentieth and twenty-first centuries. Pandemics such as the Spanish Flu of the early 20th century and COVID-19 of the early 21st century can affect people as much and possibly in similar ways as storms, eruptions, and earthquakes. The psychological, spiritual, relational, and financial impacts can be great.

---

5. Taylor, *Disaster and Disaster Stress*, 14.
6. Taylor, *Disaster and Disaster Stress*, 14.
7. Taylor, *Disaster and Disaster Stress*, 12–13.
8. Taylor, *Disaster and Disaster Stress*, 12.

Definitions and Delimitations

In any NED, infrastructural loss can affect a church and its pulpit ministry. Damaged roads or streets can prohibit parishioners from traveling. The destruction of the power grid in a region can influence a church's pulpit ministry and at least for a time affect preaching. Quarantines and stay-at-home orders can present barriers to preaching as it is usually done in a live congregational setting. Regardless of the exact character of a NED, a pastor may find oneself preaching in the context of a disaster.

SECTION TWO

Toward A Biblical View of Natural Environmental Disasters,
Or:
"Everyone talks about the weather, but . . ."

WEATHER IS A UNIVERSAL conversation topic. As a conversational topic it can be a means of connecting with another person. But for some it can be a matter of business, economy, or survival. For a farmer in any locale the weather affects everything of daily life. Unfortunately, on occasion weather has adverse and even deadly effects. Flooding, various forms of windstorms, avalanches, severe heat or cold at times are more than conversation topics—they can become natural environmental disasters. Not only weather but earthquakes, tsunamis, famines and insect infestations can be NEDs as well. From more recent experiences, disease outbreaks and pandemics may possibly qualify as NEDs with their characteristics and biological impacts being remarkably similar to meteorological and geological disasters.

A common subject of conversation both during and after a NED is that of God's involvement in such an event. Where was God during this? Did God cause this? Is God speaking in this event?

SECTION TWO

What do events such as a NED tell us about God? These are deep questions that are difficult to ignore.

Where does one look for answers? Philosophy offers explanations. Pragmaticism presents ways to cope. Pop culture sends thoughts and prayers. Some people are fully satisfied with the answers these sources offer. But if those sources and their answers prove to be unsatisfactory can wisdom be found elsewhere to deal with the effect of a NED in one's life? I believe the answer is "Yes," with the Bible not only being one of those sources but the best source. And a preacher is one who is expected to provide those answers *from the Bible*.

The biblical narrative contains many disasters of different types. Famines occurred throughout the Old Testament (Gen 12:10; 26:1-2; 41-47; Ruth 1:1, 2 Sam 21:1; 1 Kgs 18:2; 2 Kgs 4:38, Neh 5:3). Drought impacted the lives of the people both within and without ancient Israel's territory (1 Kgs 17). The plagues of Egypt involved biological eruptions (Exod 8-10) and the Philistines were stricken with an outbreak of tumors (1 Sam 5-6). Elijah's earthquake (1 Kgs 19:11) and Elisha's whirlwind (2 Kgs 2:11) illustrate environmental events as part of individuals' experiences with God.

In some NEDs recorded in the Bible, God's involvement with the event is clearly revealed though that involvement may have been different for each event. God gave guidance to Isaac by warning him not to go to Egypt during a famine as his father Abraham had done (Gen 26:1-2). Egypt certainly experienced profound NEDs in which God was directly revealed as the actor in the plagues upon Egypt (Exod 7-10). In all but the last plague of the death of the first born it can be argued that these were NEDs or NED-related. The drought and subsequent famine of Elijah's day was a result of God answering Elijah's prayer. Several times God's involvement is not recorded as a cause for a NED but as his acting to preserve creation and/or his people during a NED. He did this in Noah's Flood, Joseph's Famine, and in delivering his people during Egypt's Plagues. Later in the history of Israel God used hailstone to battle for his people (Josh 10:11).

Often when the Bible is read or studied these events are considered somewhat incidental. But when given more consideration,

SECTION TWO

the Bible's inclusion of these events in moving forward the redemption story also yields insight for one preaching in the aftermath of a NED.

The Beginning is the best place to start when considering what the Bible reveals about NEDs. The Creation Narrative of Genesis 1–2 reveals that God prepared a place for human and animal life. He both designed and provided the conditions for life with the Garden of Eden prepared especially for Adam and Eve (Gen 2:8). Concerning weather conditions, the text directly states that ". . . the Lord God had not caused it to rain on the land, . . . and a mist was going up from the land and was watering the whole face of the ground . . ." (Gen 2:5–6). Obviously, those conditions were unique from what is experienced today. As there is a hint in the biblical text that the process for watering the ground changed at Noah's Flood, it is likely that the natural dynamics that form what today is considered weather or climate were present at the beginning of the created order. When the ground was cursed by God in Gen 3, the text does not introduce any new physical laws. Rather what was natural became painful, challenging, threatening, and potentially harmful.[1]

This change can be true of weather, climate, and some biology. It is *possible* that storms, earthquakes, floods, and other phenomena that we consider out of control in NEDs were intended to a much lesser degree when God created the physical laws that cause them. Before humanity's sin, these phenomena may have been tamer. But now, in creation's cursed state, the intensity level, frequency, and the level of destruction may be the result of the curse for sin and rebellion. What may have been phenomena to maintain balance in nature's systems are now potentially destructive on occasion.

From the Creation Narrative it is logical to conclude that as Creator, God has authority over creation which includes weather, climate, and related environments. Throughout the remainder of the biblical narrative this is either restated or insinuated. The psalmists confirm that God exerts his sovereignty through weather events

---

1. To argue that death is a new physical law introduced after sin can only be made in terms of human experience. The concept of death was already present as God warned that death would be the outcome of disobedience (Gen 2:16–17; 3:3). Obviously, Adam and Eve understood what death was.

(Ps 29; 78; 107; 135). The Old Testament prophets used weather and environmental disaster imagery to communicate God's messages (Jer 51:16; Nah 1:3–7). At times, their preaching communicated blessings using weather imagery (Joel 2:23) while at other times it revealed God was acting environmentally to discipline his people (Amos 4:7).

In the New Testament the same is generally observed—weather and NEDs within the redemptive narrative with God involved in varying ways. Not only did Jesus command the weather while he was on earth, he used real and fictitous weather phenomena as sermon illustrations (Matt 7:25–27; Luke 4:25; 15:14). James referred to Elijah's historical drought-producing prayers to encourage people to pray with faith (Jas 5:17). The New Testament prophet Agabus accurately predicted a famine that occurred in Emperor Claudius' reign (Acts 11:28).

To think biblically about NEDs, one must begin with recognizing that environment and weather are certainly part of God's creation. As Creator of all things, God has authority over environment, weather, and biology. It is a way through which he cares for his creation as rain that waters the fields and crops, warmth that induces growth, and winds that cool. However, humanity's fallenness has affected creation in such a way that now disasters, outbreaks, and pandemics are also part of human experience. There are times from a human perspective that both the environment and weather are out of control. What was created for good and can still be an instrument of good, e.g. replenishing rains and refreshing winds, can now also flood, destroy, and/or kill.

CHAPTER FOUR

Noah's Flood

AFTER CREATION, THE NEXT significant story about the natural environment is Noah's Flood. A story of a great flood disaster with one man saving animal life is common in ancient literature around the world.[1] Such stories with the most similarity to the Genesis account center around Mesopotamia. The one most compared to Noah is that of Utnapishtim in the Gilgamesh Epic.[2] What is most noteworthy of these various stories is not necessarily their similarities or differences with the biblical account of Noah but the frequency of such stories across the globe and cultures. It is reasonable to deduce that these stories may be relating some human memory of an actual ancient event.

Let us do a quick flyover of the story. At the start of the pericope of Noah's flood (Gen 6:5–9:17) God sees the wicked, violent, evil condition of the earth and all flesh upon the Earth. He then announces his plan with an emphatic, "Behold I will destroy them with the earth" (Gen 6:13). God instructs Noah to build an ark and establishes a covenant with Noah and his family. After the ark's construction, Noah and his family, as his part of the covenant, enter the vessel along with the animals and food supplies.

The flood begins as the result of forty days and forty nights of continual rain. All of humanity and animal life is extinguished

---

1. Kidner, *Genesis*, 95.
2. Wenham, *Genesis 1–15*, 159.

27

SECTION TWO

except for those with Noah in the ark. After several months of a "drying out" period, Noah and his family along with their animal cargo exit the ark to begin afresh with replenishing the earth.

Noah's Flood story closes with God making a covenant promise to never again destroy all flesh with a flood of this magnitude. This promise was not only to Noah and his family but to all humanity and created life. The recurring sign of this covenant is God's bow in the clouds, commonly understood visually as the rainbow. While floods would continue to occur, none would ever destroy the earth.

While technically the beginning of Noah's Flood story is marked at Genesis 6:9, a prologue sets up the event in the verses immediately before it. Humanity's wickedness and evil intentions were the conditions that brought God to express grief. His decision to blot out people, animals, creeping things, and birds is prompted less by anger and more by grief over what has become of his creation. Old Testament commentator Derek Kidner observes from 6:13, "The Hebrew for *corrupt(ed)* (or '*destroyed*') also makes it plain that what God decided to 'destroy' (13) had been virtually self-destroyed already."[3] Old Testament scholar and theologian Walter Brueggemann offers support to this understanding of both God and Noah's Flood. He views God's posture in this event as, "God is not angered but grieved. He is not enraged but saddened."[4] God sends the flood as much as an act of cleansing as an act of judgment.

Bible commentator Gordon Wenham provides a helpful chiastic analysis of Noah's Flood pericope. According to Wenham, the narrative's schema is as follows:

> Transitional introduction (6:9–10)
>   Violence in creation (6:11–12)
>   First divine speech: resolve to destroy (6:13–22)
>   Second divine speech: "enter ark" (7:1–10)
>   Beginning of flood (7:11–16)
>   The rising flood (7:17–24)
>   God remembers Noah
>   The receding flood (8:1–5)
>   Drying the earth (8:6–14)

---

3. Kidner, *Genesis*, 87.
4. Brueggeman, *Genesis: Interpretation*, 77.

Noah's Flood

> Third divine speech: "leave ark" (8:15–19)
> God's resolve to preserve order (8:20–22)
> Fourth divine speech: covenant (9:1–17)
> Transitional conclusion (9:18–19)[5]

According to this chiasm, the central truth of the Noah Flood pericope is that God remembers Noah. Essentially, the exegetical idea is that *God acts to rescue and save his creation from the destruction that its own actions have brought about.* The story can be interpreted as God being faithful in a cleansing judgment. Whether in judgment, destruction, cleansing, or renewing God is faithful to his people; he remembers them.

This exegetical idea is not only revealing of God's character, but it has direct application for preaching in a NED. God's mindfulness for his people brings much comfort to those in relationship with him. The preacher must remember that for his own glory God's mission is the redemption of humans from their fallen relationship with him. It is especially true that those who through faith are brought into a relationship with him through Jesus Christ also draw comfort, hope, and strength from knowing that they are not forgotten by their God in disastrous times.

Additionally, Noah's Flood displays God's integrity as a covenant God. What can be misunderstood by people as capricious acts of God are instead his acting within his character toward what the circumstances warrant. As the pre-flood world was becoming destroyed due to humanity's unrighteousness, God acted righteously, justly, and correctively—all consistent with his character of faithfulness.

Something that should be noted about Noah's Flood is that a warning was given. Awareness of an approaching NED allows people opportunity to prudently prepare. God not only gave instructions to Noah to prepare but also how to prepare. Apostle Peter's writings later reveal that Noah acted as a "herald of righteousness" (2 Pet 2:5). Noah's words and/or actions announced righteousness to his generation. His preaching while building the ark essentially warned people of the natural disaster that was to come due to their

---

5. Wenham, *Genesis 1–15*, 156.

own behavior. With such a warning, would not repentance have been a prudent response to prepare for what was to come?

Noteworthy, too, of Noah's Flood story is God's care for his entire creation. Throughout the story there is insinuated an interconnectedness between humanity with the rest of creation. God's grief was due in part to what humanity's sins had done to his creation. His care is shown by his cleansing the earth while still sparing the animal species along with humankind. Since humanity's actions negatively affected the earth, God cleanses and spares both while abandoning neither.

In summation, Noah's story reveals helpful truths for when experiencing a NED. First, God remembers his people in a NED. He does not forget, ignore, or abandon them in disaster. Second, God acts in integrity with his revealed character throughout the situation. At no point in time is he ever capricious. Third, there are times when God sovereignly yet graciously provides a warning about what is coming. God warned the human population through Noah though they unfortunately did not respond. And fourth, it is true that there is an interconnectedness between humanity and the rest of creation which can produce beneficial or harmful consequences pending the actions of people.

Coaching for Preaching

Three observations from Noah's Flood can guide your preaching after a NED. You can prayerfully search the Scriptures and find ample texts not as proof texts but as proofs from the texts for each of these.

Remind people that they are not forgotten. This is our responsibility as preachers in any tragedy. Noah and the animals were not abandoned by God during the crisis. And neither is the listener of your sermons, especially one that is a follower of Jesus Christ.

Focus on the integrity of God's character. Questions can arise about the meaning of any disaster which, in turn, can prompt doubts about God. While specifics about a particular event are difficult to discern at best, listeners can be encouraged when your message is based on God's character of faithfulness and righteousness. God always acts purposefully, and your listeners likely need this truth to help them hold to God in faith. In a later chapter, we will consider Job's story and see that one can ask questions, address their doubts, and deal with negative emotions while being righteous before God.

Assure listeners of God's continual care for creation. When the nature of a crisis or disaster affects flora and fauna, it is possible that listener's pets and/or livestock, crops, and even their favorite flowers have been damaged or lost. Noah's story reassures us that God cares for all his creation. After all, we preach the Christ who told us that the Father knows the falling to the ground of every sparrow (Matt 10:29).

CHAPTER FIVE

Joseph's Famine

Joseph's life story is one that has inspired hope for generations. His was a favorite of mine as a child—and now! His story has often refreshed my confidence that God is working for my good and his glory when I cannot see it. It has fortified my patience when waiting for God to uncover what he has been doing all along.

As a preacher reading this, you know Joseph's story of how as a young man of promise and ambition he was cast away from all whom he held dear by jealous brothers. He emerged years later as the prime minister of the most powerful kingdom of his time. In between, however, was a cycle of personal disappointments that seemed to push him further into oblivion with each round. But one night, God providentially acted through a dream of Pharaoh's. Joseph's fortunes then turned. One of Pharaoh's attendants, having been a fellow prisoner with Joseph, recommended him to Pharaoh as one capable of interpreting dreams. Joseph was quickly rushed into Pharaoh's court to hear what troubled the leader.

Already known to a very small number of people as a young man with remarkable abilities and character, Joseph again displayed the amazing giftings granted him from God. By God's enablement, Joseph understood Pharaoh's dream and was able to explain to the leader what it meant—a severe famine in all the land of Egypt. He also recommended a course of actions to prepare for the famine. Pharaoh, grateful for the dream's interpretation and recognizing Joseph's unique giftings, appointed him as the one to implement the recommended plan. This elevated him to the highest position to which one could possibly be appointed in his world—second only to Pharaoh.

With Joseph's oversight, for seven years food was stored throughout Egypt in preparation for the coming famine. And after those seven years, ". . . the famine had spread over all the land" as well as "over all the earth" (Gen 41:56–57). As food shortage became starvation, people began coming to Egypt from all the earth to buy food. It was in this commerce that Joseph's story began to turn full circle.

Joseph's birth family was affected by the famine and sought Egyptian food as well. Their need for sustenance not only reunited Joseph with his family but also brought them into the borders of Egypt where they were spared throughout the famine's duration. God was providentially fulfilling his covenant to the chosen family line of Abraham.

Joseph's famine is presented in Scripture as a naturally occurring event. It was a long-sustained NED that spanned at least across a region of the world. Floods, tornadoes, snowstorms, or electrical storms seldom, if ever, have the sustained impact of a famine. Only a drought which can be the root cause of a famine can compare.

Similarities and differences exist between Joseph's Famine and Noah's Flood. Like Noah's Flood, Joseph's Famine had an advance warning. Both the flood and the famine are revealed in the texts as resolved actions on God's part. For Noah, there is an emphatic statement from God " . . . for behold, I will." Likewise, Joseph began his interpretation to Pharaoh with the words " . . . God has revealed to Pharaoh what he is about to do" (41:25). Pharaoh's dream repeating itself is interpreted as "the thing is fixed by God" (Gen 41:32). Also, in both events God acts to preserve covenant people.

There are, however, pronounced differences between the two events. First, with Joseph's Famine a covenant had been long established between God and Joseph's family. Eventually, it became understood that Joseph's separation from his family, was God acting to preserve people already in covenant with him (Gen 50:20). In Noah's Flood the covenant people that are spared are brought into covenant as part of the preparation for the flood. Second, the

SECTION TWO

non-covenantal people in Egypt responded wisely to the warning of Joseph's Famine by following his proposed plan. Unfortunately, the people of Noah's day did not repent with Noah's warning effectively ignoring the opportunity to turn. Third, Joseph's Famine, unlike Noah's Flood, was not an act of judgment or cleansing but an extreme of the regular cycles or occasions of nature. This insinuates that droughts, locust invasions, floods, tornadoes, tsunamis, earthquakes, and more can all happen as the unfortunate but normal course of nature without a deeper theological meaning or an ethical implication other than the consequences of a fallen world. And fourth, while flood and famine are both horrific to experience, the NED of Noah's Flood was a centerpiece of the narrative whereas for Joseph the famine is part of the background for the total narrative of his life.

I recognize the exegetical idea of Joseph's Famine story is that *God fulfills his covenant even in the most adverse circumstances*. Joseph certainly experienced adversity. But throughout his time in Egypt God was always with him and gave Joseph favor in everything he did. In each place with its deepening obscurity, growing distance to his young dreams, and increasing personal shame, God was fulfilling his covenant promise to Joseph's family through Joseph's circumstances. In Potiphar's house he rose to a position of stewardship; in prison he attained trusteeship; and then governorship over all of Egypt.

God's commitment to his purpose of having a people of his own is embraced by this exegetical meaning of Joseph's Famine story. On this occasion, to fulfill that purpose, the Hebrew people were protected in Egypt during a famine. This protection is one more expression of God fulfilling his covenant in adverse circumstances. God sent Joseph to Egypt ahead of his family to preserve both them and his purpose.

In the pericope of Joseph's Famine, no direct explanation for the famine is given. But this lack of a divine explanation does not mean that God was not sovereign over the event. At least five details within the story identify God's involvement and his sovereignty over the famine. First, Joseph's being in Egypt was not the course he saw his life taking as a younger man. But his being in

Joseph's Famine

Egypt was the workings of God establishing him in the right place at the right time. Second, Pharaoh's God-given dream of the famine gave warning to allow for prudent preparation. Third, the events of Joseph's life made him known to a crucial figure in Pharaoh's court—the cupbearer. Fourth, Joseph's insight regarding a course of action to prepare for the announced famine is attributed to God working in his life (Gen 40:8; 41:16). Fifth, it is in hindsight that the Bible reader can surmise that the famine was a crucial part of God's redemptive narrative. All along God was orchestrating the affairs to fulfill his mission of redemption of all who would have faith in him. God's involvement and sovereignty are on full display!

Kidner provides a very helpful application of this exegetical idea as he comments on Genesis 41:33:

> It is important to note that the impending famine, unlike many of the disasters of the Old Testament, is not a judgment. It is one of life's irregularities, and Joseph points out that a wise manager will insure against them, taking extra measures if he can see extra hazards. The principle of predictive prophecy holds good . . .: God looks for an active response. To a threat of judgment this will be repentance: to a friendly warning (Jer 38:17; Matt 24:15), realistic precautions.[1]

When God gives "friendly warning" it is to prompt preparation. As will be seen in Section Three, a warning of a NED may not change the inevitable destruction, but the psychological responses of the survivors are likely to be very different. One can potentially handle the situation in a better way when given a reasonable opportunity to prepare. When any advance warning is given for a NED, the biblically prudent response is to reasonably prepare.

Coaching for Preaching

God's fulfilling of his covenant with his people even in adverse circumstances is a preaching theme that encourages listeners after a natural disaster. As did

---

1. Kidner, *Genesis*, 195–96.

SECTION TWO

Joseph, survivors of a NED may experience cycles of disappointment as part of their recovery process. And like Pharaoh, Joseph, and all others affected by the famine, survivors may not have an explanation of why the event happened.

From the pulpit, help listeners identify specific ways God has been faithful toward them. Get permission to tell the stories shared with you as a pastor. Be as concrete as possible. Remember Pastor Clark's realization of the tipped refrigerator? For a preacher to merely say, "God was helpful for me," is not as concrete as underscoring that the appliance would have been more than one person could manage and that one can see how God was at work in the detail of which way the refrigerator fell. That is an example of a specific way of God being faithful.

Advocate planning and preparing for disaster as a sermon application. This seems counterintuitive during the aftermath of a NED. One certainly hopes to experience only one disaster in a lifetime. But the reality is that crises come in many forms, not only as natural environmental disasters. While one cannot foresee every contingency, one should be prudent. It is not only realistic to formulate a planned response to any future NED, but it is also biblical. Joseph having a plan was instrumental in God preserving his people.

CHAPTER SIX

Job's Sufferings[1]

WEATHER AND METEOROLOGICAL PHENOMENA are throughout the book of Job. Rain, snow, hail, wind, thunder, lightning (not including references of lightning as "fire"), and clouds are mentioned in sixty-one verses. In these occurrences the weather phenomena are meant either literally or figuratively. Weather activity is prominently present in God's speech to Job. The verses in God's speech literally communicate God's transcendent control of weather, environment, and climate all the while that he is immanent in the care of creation.[2] NEDs as storms, floods, and famine appear in seven verses of Job's book.

But is there any other individual whose life has been more affected by a NED than Job's life? While his sufferings began with an enemy raid upon his fields (1:15), they continued with the loss of his sheep herd and herdsmen in a lightning storm (1:16), followed by another raid which took his camels (1:17), only to be followed

---

1. Clines argues for a variant composition of Job, particularly the last speech of Elihu. See Clines, *Job* 21–37, 643–44, 887. However, I am following the traditional composition of the book of Job as published in the English Standard Version and most all modern translations.

2. In his speech to Job, God reveals his immanence poetically as commanding the morning and causing "the dawn to know its place" (38:12), seeing to it that the predator has prey for food (38:39–41), counting down the days until the mountain goat gives birth (39:1–3), and giving flying lessons to the hawk (39:26). All of these are activities of a God near and involved in his creation. See Clines, *Job* 38–42, 1090.

by the devastating loss of all seven of his sons and all three of his daughters to a "great wind" (1:19). All of this within a single day with the news of each being delivered to him in a cascade of communiques by one surviving servant from each catastrophe.

Job scholar David Clines notes that the day of Job's disaster was a day like any other day with the usual activities of his workers, his family, and himself.[3] This usual day creates the setting of Job's perspective that the events were not anticipated; no warning was given. Unlike Noah's Flood and Joseph's Famine, Job's Sufferings were unannounced and certainly unexpected. The only hint that Job may have anticipated anything aberrant was his habit of offering sacrifices for his adult children lest they had dishonored God in some way. Did he anticipate that one day something truly catastrophic would happen? Or, was he being exceptionally careful when it came to the standing of his children with God? Other than what is said in the text, Job's motives in doing this cannot be further guessed. But given his actions, it is reasonable to assume that had Job been warned of the sufferings that awaited him, he would have taken necessary precautions as the successful and prudent man that he was. As will be further elucidated later, sudden unexpected NEDs not accompanied with any warning have challenges for the survivors different from those that occur with some degree of an advance sign of their approaching.

It is significant in Job's book that at the beginning and at the end dangerous weather occurs. In the prologue, the weather is destructive and deadly which certainly gives one reason to classifying it as a NED. But at the end of the book, the weather phenomenon is a whirlwind that seems not to touch down but from which God speaks to Job. Here is a real contrast. In Satan's hands the weather devastates Job. But in the hand of God, it humbles him.

Job's friends insisted that his suffering happened as a retribution for sin. Eliphaz, Bildad, and Zophar each argue this point in some way insisting that Job must repent of whatever his sin or sins may be. They saw the world through the lenses of a principle of retribution that operates as a one-to-one correlation assuring that

---

3. Clines, *Job* 1–20, 31.

Job's Sufferings

the wicked are always punished and suffer while the righteous are always rewarded and never suffer.

This worldview of Job's friends is, inversely, that of Satan's. For Satan, a person serves God for what one gets out of it, e.g. riches, ease, notoriety, etc. For Job's friends a man that does not serve God gets pain, sorrow, and suffering. They are two sides of the same coin.

On the counterpoint to such an idea, Jewish scholar Matitiahu Tsevat states that according to Job, "No retribution is provided for in the blueprint of the world, nor does it exist anywhere in it. None is planned for the nonhuman world and none for the human world. Divine justice is not an element of reality. It is a figment existing only in the misguided philosophy with which you have been inculcated."[4] Job's friends and Tsevat are polar opposites. Job's friends see divine retribution as a one-to-one relationship—good is always rewarded, evil is always punished. Tsevat's study of Job sees no divine retribution anywhere in reality.

But I believe the truth is between these two poles. Essentially Job's story tells us that the world is not regulated by laws which assure the wicked are *always* punished in this life and the righteous *always* rewarded in this life. The truth between Job's friends and Tsevat's worldview is that *at times* in this life the wicked are punished and the righteous are rewarded. This is supported by truisms in Proverbs and God's purpose for instituting human government. However, there are also inexplicable rewards and inexplicable sufferings such as Job experienced.

A balance point between these two tensions is stated by commentator Francis Andersen, who notes that Job the man is not waiting for an afterlife for accounts to be justly settled. He concurs that for Job the book, divine retribution is not necessarily experienced in this world. Andersen states, "Rewards for virtues and punishments for vice cannot all be postponed to heaven or hell. But troubles and benefits are not distributed to mankind by an evenhanded justice, it would seem. The wicked prosper, the righteous suffer."[5] Jesus himself did not explain all accidents, tragedies, deadly

---

4. Clines, *Job 1–20*, 100.
5. Anderson, *Job*, 65.

events, or suffering. He said of his Heavenly Father while preaching the Sermon on the Mount, "For He makes his sun rise on the evil and on the good and sends rain on the just and on the unjust" (Matt 5:45).

The exegetical idea of Job, rather than answering questions about the reason for suffering, reveals that *when suffering the truly righteous remain faithful to God, continuing to trust him.* Georg Fohrer, as interpreted by Matitiahu Tsevat, understands that the problem addressed by the book of Job is not why the righteous suffer but how do the righteous respond to suffering.[6] It must be remembered that Job never was informed of the encounters between God and Satan. If Job had known them, they would likely have been as problematic for him as they are for you and me, the readers today.

Are God and Satan making a proverbial cosmic wager over the actions of just one of the beings as fickle as humans have proven to be? Is it a cosmic contest between them for Job's soul? The reader can at least see that Job's suffering is not entirely random, fickle fate. The ambiguity here points me in an entirely different direction for the exegetical idea of Job's book. I do not see the reason for Job's suffering as the book's main idea. Rather the main idea is how a faithful person responds when perplexed by suffering.

And how should the faithful person respond to suffering? One worships God at great cost recognizing that all that one has and all that one is are gifts from God. The faithful bows before God and does not accommodate one's theology to fit the situation but remains loyal to God by continuing to trust him. That does not mean, as will be seen, that the righteous cannot ask questions, have moments of being demanding, or be perplexed beyond their ability to comprehend God. But even then, they continue to trust God.

What is one to make of Job and the suffering he endured as the result of the NEDs he experienced? I offer two observations from Job's book about NEDs and then one about Job's suffering. The first observation about NEDs is that, according to Elihu and confirmed in other instances in Scripture, God uses the weather (and we can add other crisis) for lashings, land, or love (37:13). God sends severe

---

6. Tsevat, "Meaning of the Book of Job," 95.

Job's Sufferings

weather and NEDs to bring correction (lashings). This he did with a famine during David's reign (2 Sam 21). And, as its Creator he manages the climate for the sake of sustaining his land (Gen 8:22, Acts 14:17).[7] He maintains the seasons which bring needed rain, sunshine, heat, and cold. He also expresses his covenant love for creation and his people—his *hesed*—through weather. He certainly expressed *hesed* when he sent large hailstones to defeat Israel's enemies (Josh 10:6–11).

However, ascertaining acceptable specific reasons for suffering due to a specific NED—Is it for lashings, land, or love?—is likely impossible for us. Based on Satan's challenge that Job feared "God for no reason" (Job 1:9) and God's later recognition of Job's faithfulness though he was incited against Job "without reason" (Job 2:3), Drew University's Old Testament associate professor, Kenneth Ngwa's analysis of Job's prologue brings him to this observation, "Whether it is genocide or slave trade or (civil) war or terrorist attacks or deadly disease or poverty, it is abundantly clear to me that many people suffer *from and for* [emphasis his] 'causes' that are difficult to understand emotionally and intellectually, much less appropriately."[8] Whether God's purpose in a NED is for either lashing, land, or love may never be absolutely known by us. This does not mean that God ever acts purposelessly, but that his purpose is not always known by us—Is he acting for land, lashings, or love?

The second observation regarding NEDs is that from Job's book one notes that NEDs can be like a Rorschach test. You have seen such a test that we commonly call "inkblot tests." A generally undefinable inkblot on a piece of paper is shown to someone who is to respond quickly with whatever they think they see the blot to be. What one imagines the blot to be is then evaluated by the expert to gain insight into the personality and thinking of the test subject.

Just the same, an individual can experience a NED as either a test, a tribulation, and a trial or as a blessing, a benefit, and a bonus in the end. What makes the difference is whether one is looking for God's *hesed* in the experience. Ngwa, while not specifically

---

7. Anderson, *Job*, 266.
8. Ngwa, *Did Job Suffer for Nothing?*, 359–80.

SECTION TWO

addressing how one sees NEDs, well notes that the meaning of the word *barak* throughout Job must be determined in context with each appearance (1:5, 10, 11, 21, 2:5, 9, 31:20, and 42:12). The word can mean "bless" or euphemistically as "curse."[9] Does the individual "bless" God or "curse" God? Throughout his ordeal, Job argued for his innocence in opposition to his friends arguing his guilt. Even his insistence and pleading for a day in God's court to confirm his righteousness was not sinful. In the end, as he did throughout it all, he blessed God as his response to the crisis. Choosing to look for God's *hesed* can affect how one experiences a NED. In fact, I am inclined to think that this choice is among the most significant that one can make.

What can be noted from Job's suffering itself? First, Job's response in his sufferings is what is most significant about them. In all that he did or said, he did not sin (1:22, 2:10, 42:7–8). Job's initial physical reactions upon hearing the news of his losses were consistent with grief expressions of his culture.[10] Falling to the ground is not an uncommon human response to devastating news, especially that of losing a loved one. But Job's falling to the ground was more—it was prostration for worship, too. At this point Job views all that he lost including his children as having been God's gift to him.[11]

Second, it can be noted from Job's suffering that a person of faith can experience suffering and pain due to any type of evil—moral or natural—and struggle with understanding why. One can wrestle with unsatisfactory answers and ask questions of God without malice. Under such circumstances, pains, and perplexities a person can still be declared by God to be someone of integrity and righteousness. In fact, according to Job's example, while suffering one can defend their own righteousness without being self-righteous about it.

Job relieves people of faith of the feeling of guilty due to having asked why or asking where God was in their suffering. There is a distinction between asking in scorn and defiance in order to

---

9. Oswalt, "Barak," 132.
10. Andersen, *Job*, 87.
11. Clines, *Job 1–20*, 38.

prove one's argument against God, his existence and/or character; and that of asking out of genuine perplexity and pain. One can be respectful of God in one's asking. Job shows that one can actually be worshipful in and through their wrestling with what has happened.

At the end of Job's ordeal, the fact that God speaks to him is very satisfying to Job though he is given no clear explanation as to why he suffered. In the end being reassured that he had not been forgotten or ignored was sufficient for him. Being allowed to dialogue with God on a subject of God's own choosing reassured Job that God was with him and had been with him. That reassurance is what Job needed. And that is a sufficient promise especially from Jesus himself, "And behold, I am with you always to the end of the age." (Matt 28:20).

There are lessons to learn from Job regarding suffering in general and due to a NED specifically. First, how one responds to a NED is one of the most significant aspects of the event. Job chose to respond worshipfully, without blaming, and non-accusatorily. This is a noteworthy truth of Job regarding his continuing blamelessness before God. He chose to bless God and not curse him. Second, NEDs are not always explicable for those who experience them. Job had no knowledge of the dialogue between God and Satan. However, one can be assured that God is purposeful in what he does. Again, according to Elihu, God acts for lashings, land, or love; but for which reason in any given event may be beyond human comprehension or explanation. Third, Job's example encourages faithful people to pose their questions about their situation without being rebellious and incurring guilt.

Coaching for Preaching

Regarding preaching, Job's Sufferings as expounded above provides for the preacher a foundation for calling people to three potentially guilt-relieving truths. *First, the occurrence of a NED does not demand judgmental preaching.* Having suffered a NED in life does not necessarily mean with certainty

SECTION TWO

that one is being divinely punished. To preach judgment by default to victims of a NED runs the risk of placing oneself in the company of Job's friends. While it is true that God can use NEDs to correct his people and to call them to repentance, this is not necessarily true for each NED. While any disruptive life event can give pause to evaluate one's life, a NED can be just as likely inexplicable to people.

Second, encourage your listeners to look for God's hesed. How one responds attitudinally to a NED is very important. It is healthful in most every way to look for God's *hesed* in the midst of the event. In fact, this is a good life skill to utilize always, not just during a NED.

As a preacher, you have three places to look for potential displays of God's *hesed*. The first place to look is your own life. This can be an occasion for you to be appropriately transparent by sharing in your sermons what you are seeing of God's *hesed* in your own life. This can be incredibly positive for the listeners if you, too, have been victimized by the event.

The second place is others' lives. Your interaction with others will involve a lot of listening to their stories. Being alert to God's *hesed,* you will hear of these displays as you listen. As was noted in preaching coaching from Joseph's Famine, ask permission to share from others' lives their personal incidents of God's faithfulness to them in the NED.

The third place to look for displays of God's *hesed* is the corporate experience of your local church. God will be at work for the recovery of your church. For a local church, being able to see corporately God's *hesed* gives reason to rejoice in community. And noting God's *hesed* toward a local church gives reasons to those who are struggling with their own circumstances to be thankful. It also encourages, strengthens, and energizes listeners during what can be the long, tiring recovery and rebuild stages after a NED.

Third, use your preaching to encourage honest questions and guide listeners toward answers. Preaching texts from Job can show listeners that they can ask honest questions and be perplexed about a NED while remaining faithful to God. You can lift a tremendous psychological weight off listeners by preaching from Job's example of asking honest questions of one's circumstances.

While preaching, bring up hard questions in your sermon. This can help validate listeners as they likely are already thinking about these. Offer scriptural direction to help people grapple with the problem of evil, suffering, and sorrow. But in doing so, be prepared for the reality that some questions do not have answers that are satisfying to everyone. Listeners can still be encouraged by Job who remained faithful to God though he did not have his questions answered nor his suffering explained. When ministering about hard issues, especially from the pulpit, we must heavily rely upon the Holy Spirit to enable us to shepherd people onward in their relationship with God though we may not have all the answers.

CHAPTER SEVEN

Joel's Locusts

WHILE THE MAJORITY OF Old Testament prophets preached using weather imagery to communicate their messages, Joel is one of the few that preached of an actual natural environmental disaster (NED)—a locust invasion. While there are images present in Joel's book that can be suggestive of a divine or human army, I view the locust invasion of the first two chapters as an actual event. This view is based on four observations about the text.

First, the four terms Joel uses to describe the locusts—cutting, swarming, hopping, and destroying (1:4)—are commonly understood to correspond to the stages of a locust infestation.[1] Second, this being a literal locust invasion gives Joel's preaching immediacy to his nation. He is not speaking of a future event in the first two chapters but is interpreting the current events of his own time. Third, to see the locusts as other than literal is to needlessly spiritualize or allegorize the text. And fourth, Joel's use of martial images can be understood as the work of a skilled orator that presses his message upon his listeners with powerful word pictures.

Joel skillfully introduces his sermon as an historic and unbelievable announcement. "Has such a thing happened in your days, or in the days of your fathers? Tell your children of it, and let your children tell their children, and their children to another generation" (1:2b-3). This would certainly have captured the attention of his listeners.

---

1. Lewis, *Minor Prophets*, 99–100.

He then transitions to explaining the recent locust invasion (1:4). The effect of the insect horde is broad and deep. The locust affected the wine supply (1:5), the fig crop (1:7), oil from olive trees (1:10), wheat and barley (1:11), fruit trees (1:12), the food supply in general (1:16), as well as cattle and herds that were left with no pasture (1:18). The agrarian society of Joel's locale and time was greatly assaulted by the locust invasion. It resulted in losses of such magnitude that storehouses and granaries were poetically depicted as not merely empty but desolate (1:17a), torn down and dried up (1:17b). Domestic animals groaned in suffering (1:18). The forests were de-leafed (1:19) and the animals of the wilderness panted for water (1:20).

Very arresting is that Judaism as a religious practice was also battered. It resulted in the priests being unable to present grain or drink offerings because of the lack of the necessary ingredients for the offerings (1:13–14). (While the spiritual realities were vastly different, I can personally relate to the effects a NED has upon the practice of one's worship!).

The locust infestation of Joel's time was vast and intense to the degree that all of nature, humanity included, was afflicted. Like Noah's Flood, Joel's locust invasion shows that humanity and all of creation are interrelated in such a way that the actions of one affects the other. The people's neglect and rejection of God brought God's act of discipline. In this disciplinary act, not only were the people of God affected but domestic animals (1:18), the wilderness and forests (1:19), as well as wild animals (1:20) suffered. Humanity's estrangement from God caused the flora and fauna to hurt.

A significant theme of Joel's preaching is that of the Day of the Lord. This theme is not unique to him as a Hebrew prophet. However, commentator Douglas Stuart observes, "this concept is so prominent in Joel that it may be likened to an engine driving the prophecy."[2] Theologically, the Day of the Lord is an event, a very day in history, that is marked by a great revelation of God; it is a theophanic day. It entails manifestations of God and either judgment or salvation (or both). When considered across the prophetic

---

2. Stuart, *Hosea-Jonah*, 230–31.

SECTION TWO

writings of the Old Testament, Joel's description is an understatement of classic proportions, "For the day of the Lord is great and very awesome; who can endure?" (2:11). While not completely developed into eschatological implications in the Old Testament, for the prophets it is a day of divine intervention, destruction, and wrath (Isa 13:6, 9), a day of God's vengeance (Jer 46:10), as well as doom for nations (Ezek 30:3).

Joel's preaching about the Day of the Lord is critical for determining the exegetical idea of his book. Joel was preaching in a definite time of history about a definite event. The effect of the locust invasion on the nation was catastrophic to the point that its magnitude can only be grasped by the concept of the Day of the Lord. Furthermore, in the first two chapters the locusts are clearly a judgment of God that is calling for the repentance and return of his people. It is in 2:12–14 that the heart of Joel's message and the exegetical idea of the book lie—*return to God in genuine, heartfelt repentance for though he punishes with devastating actions he is gracious and merciful, slow to anger and abounding in steadfast love.* For sovereign reasons of his own, God himself relents and turns in response to human repentance.

Joel's preaching reveals that God can and does act in regard for his people in NEDs. In relation to his own people, when a NED is known to be a judgement from God, he is not acting to obliterate them. Rather it is to correct, discipline, and draw them back in repentance. And as his people repent and return, he responds out of grace, mercy, and compassion by accepting them back and blessing them with provisions for themselves and his worship.[3]

Coaching for Preaching

Joel's preaching does leave open the real possibility that a NED of any sort can be God acting in judgement calling his people back to himself. But the preacher today is not the prophet of the Old Testament regarding the receiving of direct, personal revelation from

---

3. Hubbard, *Joel and Amos*, 59.

God that has the authority of his inspired Word. This alone should temper any presumption or attempt by today's preachers to speak with such authority.

However, *with sensitivity, knowledge of the listeners, and an established relationship of trust with them, a preacher can gently encourage the examination of one's life without being judgmental.* While remembering that one does not have the authority or insight of an Old Testament prophet, preachers can gently encourage their listeners that this may be a time to give consideration to their ways and look to God who is gracious, merciful, slow to anger, and abounding in steadfast love.

Essentially, a preacher can responsibly help frame the event for listeners. I offer two suggested ways to do this for listeners without declaring the event as a judgment. *The first is to help listeners understand the event as a test of one's faith or personal faithfulness to God.* Help people understand the event as a challenge to their trusting God with what they do not understand and about so much uncertainty in their lives.

The second suggested way to frame the event is as an opportunity to consider that what has happened is uncovering any idols in their lives. Having undergone the trauma of a NED people can become introspective. It may be a season of responsiveness to the gospel for them or of evaluating the quality of their walk with Christ and their progress in sanctification. Addressing idolatry can be done gently but firmly by asking questions about where people have had their trust until now. In their education? A savings or retirement account? One's health habits? Personal survival skills? A spouse, family member or friend? You can ask about where listeners have placed their hope until now. In a potential job promotion? A future marriage? A cross-country move? A career restart?

Your context of ministry will be determinative of how you frame the event as there are countless ways. Be dependent on the Holy Spirit to give you insight for framing the event for your listeners. Actively ask and listen for his direction in prayer. And remember to present, as did Joel, that God is gracious and merciful, slow to anger and abounding in steadfast love. If he must act severely, he will also act mercifully.

CHAPTER EIGHT

Jerusalem's Famine

As in the Old Testament, NEDs—literally, figuratively, or eschatologically—are part of the New Testament. One literal event was a famine prophesied by Agabus in Acts 11. Agabus had relocated from Jerusalem to Antioch. The Antioch church was a powerful, exemplary church in Acts. Its leadership was ethnically diverse (Acts 13:1). It was a disciple-making church (Acts 11:26). It was committed to praying and fasting (Acts 13:2–3). The church experienced God's empowering presence with spiritual manifestations, particularly prophecy (Acts 11:27).

Agabus was known among the believers as one who exercised the spiritual gift of prophecy. Agabus prophetically told that there would be a "great famine over all the world" (Acts 11:28). This prophecy is to be understood as a manifestation of the Holy Spirit whereby the coming famine was supernaturally revealed to Agabus. Luke dates this famine as occurring during the reign of Claudius.

There was a series of famines in the decades of the 40s and 50s of the first century. Bruce W. Winter, Director of the Institute for Early Christianity in the Graeco-Roman World, pinpoints this prophesied famine as the one that occurred in AD 46 or 47 while Tiberius Julius Alexander was procurator of Jerusalem.[1] According to Winter, the Jerusalem church had adopted many of the time-tested Jewish synagogue practices to provide for the needs of the

---

1. Winter, *Secular and Christian Responses*, 86–106.

SECTION TWO

poor. Provisions were distributed every Friday for the synagogue widows from contributions made for such a purpose. The Jerusalem church more than likely followed this pattern except the distributions were made daily as the disciples gathered the contributions daily (Acts 2:46).[2]

Winter contrasts this with how Christians living in Greek or Roman cities would have managed a famine if in their own locale. According to Winter, even though Gentile Christians may have viewed the famine through an eschatological lens, those in Greek and Roman based cities would have, along with the other citizens, waited the appointment of a *curator annonae*. This person was a wealthy citizen that intervened in some way through management of the food supply, sharing personal food supplies that were being held for commercial interests, or perhaps directly purchasing food to be distributed.[3] There is some evidence that the "present distress" to which Paul referred in his letter to the Corinthians was one of the food shortages experienced around this time (1 Cor 7:26).[4]

The early church's response to Agabus' prophecy and subsequent famine was to provide relief for their fellow believers in Jerusalem. Individual believers were encouraged to give through their local church "according to his ability" (Acts 11:29). The relief offering was to be delivered to Judea by Barnabas and Paul (then known as Saul). The story became a subplot through others of Paul's letters as disciples in other locales were made aware of the need and urged to give generously as well. (1 Cor 16:2; 2 Cor 9:3–5; Gal 2:10).[5] As a spiritually alive church the Antioch believers quickly acted practically by sending financial help to the believers in famine-stricken Jerusalem. This gives us the exegetical idea of the brief pericope of Acts 11:27–30 as *a Spirit-filled church will respond to practical needs in practical ways.*

---

2. Winter, *Secular and Christian Responses*, 104.
3. Winter, *Secular and Christian Responses*, 86–106.
4. Winter, *Secular and Christian Responses*, 93.
5. The view that Paul actually used the collecting and sending of financial relief from pre-dominantly Gentile churches to the predominantly Jewish Jerusalem church to further cement the new bond in Christ between Jews and Gentiles is entirely compatible here.

Jerusalem's Famine

The early church's actions in this incident recorded in the New Testament are less the acts of survivors of a NED and are more the response of believers toward those who were affected by a NED. Their example is one of practical, helpful action. Antioch's first response was not to pray for their fellow believers but to give for them. How consistent with James instruction! "If a brother or sister is poorly clothed and lacking in daily food, and one of you says to them, 'Go in peace, be warmed and filled,' without giving them the things needed for the body, what good is that?" (Jas 2:15-16). An action of practical aid portrays the meaning of true saving faith— faith with works. Providing practical aid, while not precluding prayer, does express the outworking of faith.

Furthermore, it is very likely that at other times the Early Church in Greek and Roman based cities helped through some of the civic or community structures which were available to them to relieve others' needs and suffering. Winter's distinguishing how Jerusalem believers and Corinthian believers likely used different channels to help is a reasonable conclusion supported by inferences within the text. No offerings are recorded in the Bible as having been sent for Corinth or any of the other famished Greek or Roman cities in the forties and fifties.

The early church's response to the Jerusalem Famine provides an instructive example of practical action in helping relieve the needs and suffering of others, especially fellow believers. The Antioch Christians are a concrete example of how a church responded to a NED with practical help without compromising its spiritual identity by its response. While practical aid is not necessarily limited to fellow believers, it is a priority for the Church according to Galatians 6:10, "So then, as we have opportunity, let us do good to everyone, and especially to those who are of the household of faith." Prayer, spiritual counsel, emotional and psychological support are important. But for the Church practical relief, aid, and physical work are just as spiritual and necessary.

SECTION TWO

Coaching for Preaching

Drawing from the Early Church's response to the Jerusalem Famine *it is important to call people to practical acts of helping survivors.* Your preaching should provide concrete examples of how listeners can help others. This is an important sermon application throughout the recovery and rebuild time and should be made often.

In fact, sermon conclusions can include asking for commitments to specific opportunities of helping survivors recover. Calling people to practical action like clearing debris, mucking out buildings, rebuilding walls, and cooking or serving meals for workers and victims should be presented as ministry that is on par with prayer, counseling, and giving spiritual support. In this situation, the spiritual is highly practical, and the practical is highly spiritual.

Looking at the Jerusalem Famine from Winter's perspective is informative for considering cooperating or working in tandem with community and government agencies as a local church. While first responders act quickly in the immediate of a disaster, other local, state, and federal agencies over the long-term respond more slowly to survivors' needs due to what is required for them to activate. Local churches and many times denominations or humanitarian organizations can mobilize and begin working much more quickly. If your local church is unable to act corporately because of the impact the NED has had upon it, there may yet be individuals who can be encouraged by your sermon application to volunteer their energy and time to one of these other agencies.

And, by all means, do not forget to preach for people to simply help their next door neighbor in whatever way possible.

Your church, area, or region may be unaffected by a recent NED but you are aware of what has happened geographically near you. Like the churches outside the immediate area did for the believers in Jerusalem, you can arrange to send aide into the affected area. Perhaps a team of volunteers can go as many outside our area did for the Baton Rouge Flood of 2016. Many people are naturally motivated to help others in need and will want to do so. Your preaching, however, should not only move the unmotivated but shape the motivation of all that volunteer. Your sermon themes and applications preached to the congregation as the team(s) is organizing can draw from the Jerusalem Famine.

CHAPTER NINE

Further Coaching from Five Biblical Disaster Events

THE BIBLICAL DISASTER EVENTS included in the previous chapters are not exhaustive of the Bible text. But they provide a foundation to begin building a framework for biblically understanding disasters and for preaching in the aftermath one. From the preaching consideration drawn from the five chosen biblical NEDs, some coaching points for preaching after a NED can be developed.

Addressing a natural environmental disaster from both the pulpit and in conversations is to be done with much humility. Humility for the situation comes in recognizing that, first, only God is omniscient. God's omniscience should humble a preacher. Job realized that his knowledge of the events of his own life was incomplete when he was before God. And God never explained to Job why he experienced what he did. God alone is omniscient, and an effective preacher recognizes this.

Humility also recognizes that others may know more than you. One's knowledge is not only incomplete before an omniscient God, but also possibly before someone with whom one is having a conversation. The other person may have more experience with NEDs. It is likely that someone listening to your sermon may be more knowledgeable or be better educated than you about disaster-related issues. This would especially be so if relief workers, volunteers, first responders, civic leaders, etc. are present for a sermon.

Further Coaching from Five Biblical Disaster Events

Third, humility recognizes that powerful forces of nature can overwhelm all forms of human strength. Who can out swim rushing torrents through gorges? Who can safely sail through a tsunami with no loss or damage? Who can build an indestructible structure? What civic leader or policy maker can manage the innumerable scenarios within even one NED? What economic power can continue to rescue, rebuild, restore, and resuscitate? What preacher can minister to the needs of NED survivors in their own power and might? Nature's forces can be overwhelming of everyone. Humility enables one to accept the limits of human strength and power that natural environmental disasters overpower.

When in the pulpit, show humility by appropriate transparency regarding your own victimization by the disaster. Present yourself more as a fellow sufferer not as a rescuer. And do not be the "chief sufferer" either. A humble preacher will be aware of one's tone and vocabulary while preaching. Loud volume with intensity may not be appropriate; the point can be better heard and accepted by the listener when spoken in a soft tone. Harsh words have little if any place when addressing listeners that have experienced the trauma of a disaster.

Humility aids compassion toward those who are devastated by what has happened to them. It helps the preacher not to be an "answer man" and instead be an "available man" who listens and attempts to provide for other's immediate needs. Your being available to others is communicated from the pulpit by having been engaged and involved with the people before entering the pulpit.

When in conversations with others, humility is shown in the preacher who actively listens to the survivors' stories. While the stories one hears may provide good material for preaching, to listen for only that purpose shows disrespect to the survivors. Interest must be genuine. Just as one does not presume the ability to totally relate to a person in grief, so one does not assume that they know exactly how a survivor feels.

Remind your listeners that God created the natural laws and dynamics involved in environmental disasters though those are now marred due to humanity's sin. Weather is God's idea. Rain, snow, wind, and sunshine are all part of his creation that he deemed

SECTION TWO

good. his deeming them good at creation means that they met his intended purpose for their existence. What is now experienced as a NED is part of the painful consequence of humanity's fallenness. As the Creator, God certainly has final authority over tectonic plates, volcanic pressures, the weather, climate and the dynamics that form them. But as Apostle Paul wrote to the Romans, creation itself is presently in the bondage of decay awaiting the fullness of freedom of the children of God (Rom 8:20, 22).

Let us not forget that we as humans are affected by our fallenness and our being dead in sin before being born again. As fallen beings our understanding of life and others, our decisions, and the policies we formulate are just some of the ways we are both tainted and tainting of what is around us. In light of our fallenness consider this—before the Fall, humanity may have possessed the wisdom and the will to structure our lifestyles, economies, and living conditions that would not assume irresponsible risks such as living in potentially perpetual danger zones. Perhaps we would have naturally loved others in a way as not to allow economical forces or other reasons to motivate someone to take those risks.[1] We may have lived in a way that the effect of NEDs (if not the NEDS themselves) would have been greatly mitigated. This is something worth the consideration.

Aside from the above speculation, your sermons should be informed by these two truths: one, God created everything and deemed it good; and two, everything is marred by sin and human fallenness. Helping listeners grasp that the world we now live in is a broken world will not soothe all hurts. But it is a helpful truth especially when coupled with God's promise of a new Heaven and a new Earth in which such events and suffering will not be present.

Be extremely guarded against confidently assigning judgment as the meaning of a natural disaster. Judgmentalism is not helpful in the immediate aftermath of such an event. People need comfort, hope, and strength. There may eventually be a time to consider that

---

1. For a good argument for how a natural environmental disaster (Hurricane Katrina in 2005) was not only a natural disaster but a human-caused disaster based on generations of racism, economic disparity, and foolish building see Duke et al., *Natural Disasters*, 56–70.

Further Coaching from Five Biblical Disaster Events

there are occasions in history when God does act with cleansing judgment like with Noah's Flood. But as he did through Joel's Locusts, it is to call people to repentance—especially his people.

Encourage your listeners with the truth that a righteous person can ask questions, struggle with acceptance of events, and experience negative emotions while remaining faithful to God. Job certainly displayed this. Which is more faithful—to deny one's emotions, avoid being intellectually honest, walking through life passively in circumstances while claiming trust in God; or, to acknowledge one's fear, anger, and confusion, to wrestle with questions that seem to have no answers, to be aggressive in responding to events and yet choosing to trust God who perplexes you at least in the moment if not for a lifetime? Preaching such a view from the pulpit lifts a sense of needless guilt believers may have when they recognize they are questioning, struggling, and feeling negative emotions like anger. Sermons that include or have as their main text psalms of lament and imprecation can help the listener know how to work through their struggle with these realities without defaming or cursing God.

Your sermons preached in the aftermath of a disaster should include calls for practical service as one way to motivate the loving of others. Point out opportunities to serve and display God's compassion to people. Preaching should include calling survivors not directly affected by the disaster to serve those who have been affected. As the restoration process proves to be long-term, preaching needs to become more encouraging and motivating for service. However, such preaching should not browbeat when recovery and restoration periods prove to be longer than anticipated.

Australian researchers Aaron Ghiloni and Sylvie Shaw identified this guideline in their study of the Queensland Floods of 2011. In the early part of that year "floods claimed 35 lives, caused $30 billion dollars in damage, covered three-quarters of the state, and severely affected two-hundred thousand people across seventy cities and towns."[2] The authors observed a "priority of the practical" among the believers or churches. One local pastor is quoted as exemplifying this, "Sunday is a so-called sacrosanct day for Christian

---

2. Ghiloni and Shaw, "'Gumboot Religion,'" 28

worship. We said, 'no.' We shut our services down and said, 'Come on, get your gumboots and pick up a shovel and away we go.'"[3]

Obviously, many survivors can be in a difficult position to act on such application. Remember that one is only responsible to share what they have, not what they do not have. But as the Macedonian church delighted Paul with their giving out of their need, the same can be repeated in many events by many believers.

Repeat often in your preaching and in personal conversations that God remembers his people and his promises. Individual survivors can feel overlooked and forgotten if no friends check on them though the friends are as occupied with recovery as they are. Some may feel neglected by family. All can easily think they are forgotten when insurance, government aide, or mortgage companies are slow to act. Entire communities can similarly experience this when there has been little news coverage, or they live in an overlooked or inaccessible area.

Recurring throughout the biblical disaster events referenced earlier is the theme of God remembering. From Noah's rescue in the flood to the Early Church's efforts to aide those in famine-stricken areas, God's commitment to his people is seen. The ancient prophets preached such messages when interpreting the events of their day as God's judgment. Their messages were calls to repentance coupled with divine promises of forgiveness and restoration by a God who is merciful and mindful.

---

3. Ghiloni and Shaw, "'Gumboot Religion,'" 31–32.

SECTION THREE

Effects of a Natural Environmental Disaster Upon the Survivors, Or: "Who are these people I'm preaching to?"

COMMUNICATORS, ESPECIALLY HOMILETICIANS, EMPHASIZE the importance of knowing one's audience.[1] John Stott's metaphor of the preacher as a bridge builder crossing the gulf between the world of the text and the modern world implies that the preacher know his world well enough to place the footings of the bridge in the modern world.[2] Knowing the lifestyles, interests, educational levels, economic statuses, cultural backgrounds, marital statuses, age, worldviews, and other points by which many people are identified helps the preacher in many ways. Perhaps the most significant help the preacher receives by knowing his audience is in the area of application. Bringing the exegetical idea of a biblical text to bear upon the daily lives of people is at the heart of effective preaching.

A pastor in a local congregational setting is at a great advantage in knowing the listeners attending the worship service. Over time,

---

1. Liftin, *Public Speaking*, 39; Keller, *Preaching*, 93–120; Kim, *Preaching with Cultural Intelligence*, 5.
2. Stott, *Between Two Worlds*, 137.

SECTION THREE

a local pastor learns the individuals of the congregation. Knowing the plight of a single mom, being aware of the loneliness of the widower, and remembering the student starting a new school year are all important knowledge when developing sermon application.

Knowing the congregation's corporate persona gives an advantage as well in communicating. A local church's values, specific doctrinal beliefs, and its sense of mission not only enhance a preacher's ability to communicate but also to specifically apply biblical texts to that local body. This is not automatic, but it is natural for a pastor who regularly and authentically interacts with parishioners in the course of regular pastoral ministry.

Understanding the unique culture of the church's community setting can be immeasurably helpful, too. Knowledge of one's community is not only helpful for weekly preaching but especially if asked to address the local community at large after a disaster. Such an opportunity may be a funeral, a civic assembly, or a community service sponsored by area churches. Pastors understand the role that funeral services fill in helping the bereaved. Preaching a funeral due to an unexpected or tragic death is similar to preaching a funeral as part of the aftermath of a natural disaster. But attendees from the community that typically are present to be supportive of the bereaved family will likely themselves be grieving a plethora of their own losses due to the disaster.

Public assemblies called for by civic or spiritual leaders are often part of helping a community to heal, be resilient, and to recover. Community gatherings in these circumstances can be very morale building for a community. These are situations where knowledge of the listeners can potentially increase one's preaching effectiveness.

The knowledge that a local pastor has about people, a church, and a community usually grows over time of service in that locale. This makes a strong case for the relationship between long-term pastorates and fruitfulness or effectiveness. But after surviving a disaster individuals, local churches, and communities can be different not only because of who or who is not in attendance, but because of what they have experienced. A pastor needs knowledge of these potential differences. This section addresses how surviving a NED affects people, churches, and communities. The degree of these differences and their manifestations are affected by three variables—a warning about the disaster, personal resiliency, and individual robustness.

A warning of coming winds, waves, or other storms gives an opportunity for people to prepare or possibly avoid immediate danger. With a warning one may move out of the way of the approaching disaster, take actions to mitigate some of the effect of the disaster, or both. A warning can shape people's perceptions of what is about to happen or has happened by giving them some sense of control amid the chaos of a disaster. A sense of control better positions people psychologically for the aftermath.[3] Of the five biblical disasters considered earlier, three were preceded with a warning.

Another variable to people's response is resilience. Environmental trauma expert, Darlyne Nemeth of the Louisiana State University, defines resilience as ". . . the ability to be firmly grounded in today, to benefit from yesterday, so that we can see ourselves in tomorrow. This requires faith."[4] This quality, if present, seems to be imbedded in an individual.[5]

Not all people possess this quality. Those who lack resiliency are characterized as having "little hope, . . . little joy, . . . little charity. They live only for today; bemoan the past; and they see nothing but despair ahead."[6] Without resilience, people tend not to survive the trauma of a disaster either physically or emotionally.[7] Fortunately, resilience can be developed.[8]

The third variable to people's response to a disaster is their robustness. Robust people are "strong, powerful, vigorous, and healthy individuals. They find ways to survive, adapt, and change in order to meet the challenges."[9] It is further observed that robust individuals tend to rise to leadership or influence in the aftermath

3. Halpern and Tramontin, *Disaster Mental Health*, 28.
4. Nemeth, January 31, 2019, email message to the author.
5. Walker and Heffner as quoted by Nemeth and Whittington, "Our Robust People," 116.
6. Nemeth and Whittington, "Our Robust People," 116–17.
7. Nemeth and Whittington, "Our Robust People," 117.
8. Aten and Broan, *Spiritual First Aid*, 11.
9. Nemeth and Whittington, "Our Robust People," 118.

SECTION THREE

of a NED.[10] Robust people can by physically strong and energetic, mentally tough, as well as emotionally stable in the midst of chaos and crisis. It is obvious that this quality will be a determining factor for how a person is affected by a disaster.

The chapters in this section first look at how NEDs can affect individuals physically, psychologically, sociologically, and spiritually. Next the affects upon a community at large are considered. Chapter 15 is how churches as corporate bodies experience NEDs just as do individual people. The concluding chapter is further coaching for preaching with these affects in mind.

---

10. Nemeth and Whittington, "Our Robust People," 118.

CHAPTER TEN

The Physical

WHILE INDIVIDUALS RESPOND TO a disaster in their own unique way, there are common experiences among individual survivors. One area of commonality is the physical. The human body can react to what has happened in many ways. One can experience heart palpitations, breathing challenges, immediate and longer lasting digestive issues as well as headaches and general body pain.[1]

During the moments of the disaster and immediately following a person likely experiences an *acute stress response*.[2] This is commonly talked about as a "fight or flight" reaction. It is an automatic physiological response where the body increases the heart rate which in turn increases the blood flow to the brain, heart, and lungs, as well as the major muscle groups. Conversely, the digestive system experiences constricted blood flow. Blood pressure increases, stored sugars are released, adrenaline and other hormones are added to the blood stream, blood-clotting agents are released in anticipation of injuries, and pupils dilate. In this state a person is physically ready to quickly move from danger or confront the coming forces of nature.[3]

If a person's body prepares for such a scenario but does not expend the energy as expected it adversely affects a person's

---

1. Halpern and Tramontin, *Disaster Mental Health*, 83.
2. Halpern and Tramontin, *Disaster Mental Health*, 81.
3. Halpern and Tramontin, *Disaster Mental Health*, 82.

SECTION THREE

physiology and psychology. The released sugar and tensing of muscles convert to lactic acid producing muscle soreness and/or cramps. The hormones intended to help the person focus instead can incite aggression, frustration, irritation, cause difficulty in concentration, feelings of anxiety and fear, depression, and withdrawal.[4] All of this in turn produces fatigue.

When a person does expend all the energy created by the body's "fight or flight" reaction they can still be physically *tired* by moving/fleeing from harm's way. By tiredness I mean the need for rest in the immediate hours or days after a natural disaster. The degree of challenge that moving/fleeing may pose can depend upon several factors. The terrain and distance traversed to reach safety, obstacles encountered, mode of transportation or movement, and pacing are just some of the factors that figure into how tired one will be. An individual's health and/or fitness greatly factor into the physical effects one experiences, especially regarding tiredness and fatigue.

One may be physically impacted by *deprivation* both in the immediate and in the long-term. There may be no opportunity for adequate rest or sleep for some time after a disaster strikes. It is not unusual for individuals to be without food or have a limited supply of food. Lack of adequate drinking water is typical and potable water may not be available for several days or longer. Necessary or helpful medication may no longer be at hand. A safe place to shelter during a natural disaster may not be found. Buildings and structures can quickly be rendered unsafe for occupation or entirely destroyed due to the damaging power of nature that contributes to no opportunity to safely rest.

The possibility of *injury* in a disaster is very great. It is inherent for a disaster that damage is not limited to structures and terrain but can include the human body. The chances of being burned, choked, cut, or suffering breaks is likely increased. Exposure to chemical or nuclear hazards can be a risk. Germ-infested surroundings can be threatening. Some injuries may not quickly or easily heal.

Long-term fatigue is a real possibility. If search and rescue is immediately needed, then fatigue and possible deprivations can be

---

4. Halpern and Tramontin, *Disaster Mental Health*, 82.

more intense. During recovery and rebuilding, which can last for many months if not years, physical fatigue can be ongoing. In both the immediate aftermath and long-term recovery, a person may try to be as productive and functional in life as they were before the event. But now without the support of the familiar or of routines, life's responsibilities are more difficult to fulfill. This can add to a person's physical fatigue.

Coaching for Preaching

Always keep in mind that you are preaching to tired people. Give consideration to shortening the sermon length. Listeners' expressiveness or indicators of response to your sermon may not be as evident as under normal circumstances. Do not let this lesser responsiveness be personally discouraging. Your listeners may be receiving the message very well but be subdued in their expressiveness due to fatigue.

Communicate as simply as possible so listeners can more easily follow the sermon. Due to tiredness and fatigue it may be difficult for listeners to concentrate. Being as concrete and as concise as possible in preaching can be helpful.

Consider adjusting the time given to each of the elements of the worship service. The overall length of the service can be shortened allowing the people to use the time personally to either rest or attend to the many details involved in rebuilding their lives. If choosing realistically to adjust the length of the sermon or service duration do not succumb to allowing the sermon to become only a devotional thought and the service to be merely a quiet time. During the crisis, people need the Word of God and the power that it brings into their lives.

CHAPTER ELEVEN

The Psychological

THE PSYCHOLOGICAL EFFECTS OF a disaster upon individuals can be profound. The World Health Organization, specifically citing a study of earthquake victims in China, reported in 2001 that studies of victims of natural disasters show a "high rate of mental disorders."[1] Nemeth and Whittington identify what seems to be a universal six-stage process following a NED.[2]

This universal six-stage process begins with *shock*. Shock is "a reaction to a sudden physical or mental disturbance; a state of profound mental and physical depression consequent upon severe physical injury or emotional disturbance."[3] Shock in these circumstances affects the way a person thinks and makes decisions. It is not unusual that heroic feats are done due to shock—acting on impulse without considering the risks or potential consequences of one's actions.[4] Shock can also affect a person in an entirely different way essentially shutting them down with indecision or temporary physical collapse.

The second stage is *survival mode* in which people do whatever it takes to survive. Venezuelan psychiatrist Guillermo Garrido suggests that there are five types of victims in the survival stage:

  1. World Health Organization, "Burden of Mental and Behavioral Disorders," 44.
  2. Nemeth and Whittington, "Our Robust People," 120–26.
  3. Campbell, *Psychiatric Dictionary*, 667.
  4. Nemeth and Whittington, "Our Robust People," 121.

The Psychological

1. "Those who are overwhelmed and in shock due to the emotional impact of the trauma."
2. "Those who tell their horrifying story while displaying no emotions."
3. "Those who feel guilty for surviving while others have died or were injured."
4. "Those who believe they a) made the disaster worse somehow, b) could have done something to help, c) could have prevented it from happening, or d) could have saved someone."
5. "Those who have been victims of group violence."[5]

While this information relates to diagnosis by professionals, it does give a preacher further insight into a sermon listener's possible experience.

The third stage is *assessment of basic needs*. These needs include food, water, shelter, safety, and addressing medical issues. Provisions and shelter can be sporadic immediately after a disaster. Governmental agencies, non-governmental aid organizations, and benevolent citizens in the area need time to respond to the crisis. That chronological lag can make adequate provisions scarce or rare for at least the short term.

The fourth stage is *awareness of loss* which involves surveying the damage. While looking for lost property is part of this stage, it is finding lost loved ones that usually transitions survivors. Helpful to the survivors in stage four is acknowledgement of their pain by an authority figure.[6] Visits to an area struck by a NED from state officials, community leaders, and company CEOs invoke a settling experience that "allows people to face their personal losses."[7] To this list of authority figures should be added local pastors in visiting or contacting their parishioners. If you as a local pastor are also victimized by the event with all the added responsibility that that

---

5. Guillermo Garrido quoted by Nemeth and Whittington, "Our Robust People," 122.

6. Guillermo Garrido quoted by Nemeth and Whittington, "Our Robust People," 125.

7. Guillermo Garrido quoted by Nemeth and Whittington, "Our Robust People," 125.

entails, perhaps other church leaders such as elders, deacons, or small group leaders can help make affirming contact.

Stage five is *susceptibility to spin and fraud*. Spin and fraud can take many forms and can be perpetrated by many different people and agencies, including governmental agencies. While such people and agencies can be acting with any number of motivations, the survivors of a natural disaster are vulnerable to further victimization in this stage.

The last stage is *resolution*. This stage can last months or years. According to Nemeth and Whittington, this stage usually begins at the first anniversary of the event and is marked by a reaction to the event such as an emotional regression.[8] Symptoms of reacting to the event's anniversary can be "constant worry, irritability, tension, headaches, restlessness, sleep disturbance, sadness, and fatigue."[9]

Another psychological effect of a natural environmental disaster is *disorientation and the role of "place."* After a natural disaster one's possessions may not be where they once were, routes and highways may be gone or at least impassable, and the simplest routines of life are disrupted forcing one to rethink how to function. Relationships can be affected by disorientation, also. Since homes, workplaces, schools, hospitals, worship facilities, the geography of a locale can all be altered or destroyed in a natural disaster, the effect of disorientation and the significance of the role of place can become intertwined.

The feeling of disorientation is due in part to the role that 'place' has in people's lives. Place is intrinsic to the divinely created order. God created a place for Adam and Eve as humans, a place that was home for them. When God revealed himself to Abram and formed a covenant with him, he promised a place for Abram and his family. In the history of the ancient people of God in the Old Testament their homeland played a weighty role in their story.

Modern sociology and psychology also recognize that place has a role in people's lives. Research data is growing that notes a human-nature relationship or connection. For example, studies

---

8. Nemeth and Whittington, "Our Robust People," 126.
9. Nemeth and Whittington, "Our Robust People," 126.

The Psychological

show that children with attention deficit hyperactivity disorder improve in cognitive function when in a natural park setting. Alzheimer's patients are positively affected by simply having a view of a garden through their window. Recovery from depression has also been observed when a depressed person is in contact with nature.[10]

A theory has been formulated from these observations—*Biophilia*. Biophilia is the hypothesis that people "... show an affinity for other forms of life and therefore, by extension, the natural world in general."[11] This theory contains the view that both individuals and communities have a "sense of place" which is "a feeling of belonging to a particular geographic place that is supported by familiarity with and fondness for the features and creatures of the place."[12] Biophilia theorizes what is commonly observed and sensibly stated—people that live in mountainous areas are fond of mountains; those living near the beach like the ocean.

While a Christian preacher may not agree with the evolutionary aspects of Biophilia as a theory, one can agree biblically and experientially that place is important for people. And, a disaster can affect, even rupture, the bond people have with their place causing psychological stress. This is part of the loss experienced in a disaster.

A sense of place is also more than a relationship with the natural world. Psychologists offer that a home expresses the resident's individual identity and cultural bond. It is recognized that worldwide people use their homes simultaneously to "make themselves distinct from others" all the while they "design, decorate, and use their homes in ways that portray their communality and ties to their neighbors and culture."[13] The strength of bond between people and place is brought to the forefront by the straight-forward question, "If individuals are not invested in their communities, why would so many remain in settings where floods, earthquakes, tornados, and

---

10. Zelinski, "Our Critical Issues," 170.
11. Zelinski, "Our Critical Issues," 170.
12. Zelinski, "Our Critical Issues," 171.
13. Gauvin et al., "Homes and Social Change," 184.

so forth are real threats—or build in the same area after seeing their homes destroyed?"[14]

The role of place is very specific to a survivor's home which is ideally one's haven. It is there where shared mealtimes bond the family and to where one retreats from daily demands. After a natural disaster, this haven may no longer exist for them or is drastically altered. Familiar patterns and routines for daily activities are lost and cause disorientation. The route for driving to work, which stores one regularly shops without needing to think about it, how much time it takes to traverse town; and even within the buildings one occupies such as knowing where one's classroom is located, in which drawer is kept the spoons, or where to leave one's car keys at night—all are routines that when disrupted to the degree of a NED's aftermath can be disorienting.

Of the psychological impacts experienced in a NED, perhaps none are as emotionally and relationally painful as *loss and grief*. Loss and grief can be wide-ranging, but none is as significant as the loss of a loved one. Halpern and Tramontin helpfully distinguishes loss and grief that is produced by a disaster. Traumatic loss is experienced at the death of a loved one in a disaster. The sudden, possibly horrific, violent circumstances of the death deepen the pain.[15] Traumatic grief, sometimes called traumatic bereavement, "is the process of dealing with traumatic loss."[16] Traumatic loss and traumatic grief share the characteristics of any loss and grief but "is often compounded and made more complex by a shared, communal context, as in disasters."[17]

Compounding the hardship and complexity of the loss of a loved one in a disaster may be the complications of recovering a loved one's body. It is possible that a survivor may not have confirmation of a death for some time after the disaster. It is commonly recognized that having a body for confirmation of death as well as for ceremonies and rituals is needful for closure for survivors. The

---

14. Shumaker and Taylor, "Toward a Clarification of People-Place Relationships," 222.
15. Halpern and Tramontin, *Disaster Mental Health*, 90.
16. Halpern and Tramontin, *Disaster Mental Health*, 90.
17. Halpern and Tramontin, *Disaster Mental Health*, 90.

The Psychological

locating and recovering of bodies can be very traumatic in and of itself. The condition of the body once recovered can compound the loss for the survivor. And given the communal context when death has been widespread, funeral services and death ceremonies may be delayed due to the limited resources available within the affected community.

Suicide may also compound the complexity of the loss of a loved one. Epidemiologist and associate professor at Rafsanjan Medical School, Iran, Mohsen Rezaeian states that there is a theoretical connection between exposure to natural disasters and suicidal behavior. He notes that a number of studies make the connection between the two.[18] These can mean that suicides may increase after a disaster.

The wide range of loss and grief includes physical loss (tangible loss) and symbolic loss (more abstract).[19] A disaster survivor can experience both types which includes "pets, property, a way of life, occupation, a sense of invulnerability, self-esteem and identity, future hopes, and trust in God or protective powers."[20] But the grief experienced as symbolic loss "is often repressed, denied, or postponed because it pales in a comparison to the more penetrating loss of life. And the psychological, symbolic, intangible losses—those that shatter the individual's assumptions about the world—may be even more readily submerged."[21] It can be readily seen that traumatic grief, while having parallels with normal grief, can also be very distinct and may not follow the grieving patterns most pastors and preachers are accustomed to seeing in ministry.

Disaster survivors can also experience the loss of the sense of oneself. Psychologists see that a person's self-conception or identity is formed over time but "trauma disrupts the meaningful organization of the self and the world leaving people feeling helpless, hopeless, and worthless."[22] One's self-conception before living through

---

18. Rezaeian, "Adverse Psychological Outcomes," 289.
19. Halpern and Tramontin, *Disaster Mental Health*, 90.
20. Halpern and Tramontin, *Disaster Mental Health*, 90.
21. Halpern and Tramontin, *Disaster Mental Health*, 93.
22. Halpern and Tramontin, *Disaster Mental Health*, 106.

a natural disaster and the reality of one's actions, attitudes, and/or statements made both during and after the disaster can be incongruent. One may have considered themselves resilient and robust only to discover that they were neither while in the crisis. A Christian that perceives themselves as spiritually mature may be more than surprised by their conduct and character as they are tested by what has happened. At the same time one may discover that they are more mature and stronger than they had previously considered themselves to be. If there is a pronounced difference between one's original self-conception and the reality of one's conduct, a survivor will need to incorporate this new information about themselves and reconstruct their self-conception.

A natural environmental disaster can also result in the loss of one's culture. Communities tied to their location such as fishing villages, resort and tourist destinations, farming areas, centers of political or economic power are just some of the communities that can be changed in moments by a natural disaster. Not only the event itself but the rate of loss—in a few seconds in some cases—can compound the trauma. At times, people are forced to relocate and/or alter their lifestyles after a natural disaster.[23] Nemeth and Whittington make the case that efforts of Hurricane Katrina survivors that insisted upon rebuilding the Lower Ninth-Ward, a low-lying, poverty-prone area, did so out of the desire to reestablish and preserve culture. They write, "We can survive the loss of loved ones, for we know how to grieve. We can survive the loss of property, for we know how to rebuild. But we cannot emotionally survive the loss of culture."[24]

Survivors of disasters experience a *range of emotions and emotional reactions*. People are distressed, can feel overwhelmed, can be irritable and impatient. A panicked episode is not uncommon.

My experience of interacting with people both immediately and for many months after the Baton Rouge Flood of 2016 indicates that the three most common emotions post-event are anxiety, anger, and depression. Anxiety manifested in the middle

---

23. Gauvin et al., "Homes and Social Change," 186.
24. Nemeth and Whittington, "Our Robust People," 125.

The Psychological

of the first week after the Baton Rouge Flood. There were fearful conversations among citizens Wednesday evening, August 17, 2016, when an area rainfall occurred that was officially recorded at 3.81 inches.[25] As it rained and some areas had trouble shedding the water, many wondered if another flood was about to happen. Also, during the rebuilding phase, concerns regarding policies and decisions of FEMA caused much anxiety. Furthermore, unclear FEMA regulations and inconsistent communication created anxiety over unknown long-term consequences of decisions owners had to make about their property.

Anger is another emotion that can be felt and can be directed at any number of subjects. Some people in the Baton Rouge Flood were angry that the event itself happened. I observed such anger as a vague emotional undercurrent in people's daily activity and interactions. Still others were angry at God or angry about decisions they or others made which they considered contributing factors to their own experience of the flood. As recovery transitioned into rebuilding, frustrations with shortages of materiel, skilled labor, credible contractors, delays, and the length of time taken to rebuild all fueled anger. Insurance companies were the objects of anger. Local, state, and federal governments were an inducement of much anger. Lack of information, poor communication of requirements, permits and codes, the amount and redundancy of reporting frustrated people. Unfortunately, anger can not only be acute but become chronic in the aftermath of a disaster.

Depression is also a common emotional response following a natural disaster. People are grieving over various losses of many different types. Loved ones, property, wealth, sentimental but important mementos such as family heirlooms, wedding pictures, love letters, and baby keepsakes can all be taken away. In the Baton Rouge Flood the unanticipated time for recovery and rebuilding created a sense of hopelessness for some people. All of this can contribute to a loss of hope which underscores depression about what has happened or the seemingly unending process of recovery.

---

25. National Weather Service, "Baton Rouge Ryan, LA. August 17, 2016."

SECTION THREE

Someone challenged by clinical depression before a disaster can find that their struggle is multiplied by a NED.

Extreme psychological issues can be experienced after a natural disaster. In December 2009 a tsunami struck southeastern India killing almost three million people and leaving one million homeless. Studies revealed that 12 to 40% of the population in the Tamil Nadu area were affected with post-traumatic stress disorder (PTSD).[26] The American Psychiatric Association website defines PTSD as "a psychiatric disorder that can occur in people who have experienced or witnessed a traumatic event such as a natural disaster."[27] While the diagnosis of PTSD is the work of mental health care professionals, it is helpful as a preacher to be aware that some listeners may be dealing with its core symptoms of hyperarousal (being extremely vigilant and alert), reexperiencing (flashbacks, nightmares), and avoidance (trying to avoid reminders of the trauma).[28] What may be more commonly observed as a pastor is Acute Stress Disorder (ASD). ASD shares symptoms with PTSD but is shorter in duration and intensity. According to the *Diagnostic and Statistical Manual of Mental Disorders, 5th Edition*, the symptoms of ASD last from three days to one month. This duration is an important distinguishing feature between ASD and PTSD.[29]

Coaching for Preaching

The ways an individual, a church, and/or a community is impacted by a NED often overlap and interact with one another. The mere reality that a natural disaster is a physical event that affects people psychologically speaks of that. While these affects often vary among individuals, preaching the Word

---

26. Zelinski, "Our Critical Issues" 175.

27. American Psychiatric Association, "What is Posttraumatic Stress Disorder?"

28. Halpern and Tramontin, *Disaster Mental Health*, 115.

29. *American Psychiatric Association: Diagnostic and Statistical Manual of Mental Disorders*, 281.

The Psychological

of God—the gospel—can positively influence everyone. God's eternal truth is first and foremost a message of reconciliation between us and him, but it can also be therapeutic, encouraging, enlightening, and empowering to people.

Trust the power of God's Word to positively affect people as it is preached. The disaster need not interrupt consistently and sequentially expounding the Bible. There may be occasions during the recovery and rebuilding that it is wise if not necessary to pause an expositional sermon series to address immediate pressing needs. But even that should be done as exposition from Scripture.

Preach sermons that aim to reassure people. Reassurance is a helpful theme for application to the psychological affects upon survivors. As the listeners' world has become unfamiliar and disorienting, God's eternality and faithfulness are reassuring truths. Reassurance of God's keeping power and ready forgiveness is a helpful theme for listeners struggling with their own failures and/or those of others. Plainly and simply preach that God forgives. Proclaim God's restorative power and the wisdom in Scripture about relationships. This is a tool for strengthening people's connection with God and one another.

Address sorrow and grief in sermon application. Comfort from God's Word is greatly needed in the context of a disaster's potential psychological effects. Whether in a funeral service or in a regular gathering for worship, remember that mourning people are very likely to be present. They may be mourning the loss of people, things, a sense of safety, a loss of their

SECTION THREE

sense of self, community, and possibly culture. From the Psalms and the lives of Old Testament people, permission can be given to the listeners to mourn over all their losses including the loss of people.

Preach about God's unchangeable nature. The listeners are experiencing great and undesired change in their lives. With the possible impact upon the listener's culture, the potential need to relocate, or being required to learn a new job skill set due to affected industries, the listener has need of confidence in God's faithfulness, his abiding involvement in the lives of his people, and belief in God's unchangeableness.

Preach about emotions. Preaching that helps the listener sort through and manage their emotions truly ministers. Considering that anxiety, anger, and depression are quite common emotional responses to a natural environmental disaster, the psalms of lament can be a great source for preaching texts to address these emotions. The Bible is replete with references to anxiety and fear. These should be utilized from the pulpit. When dealing with anger, the imprecatory psalms provide modeling for healthy ways to deal with one's anger without harming others. The Psalms, passages from Job and Jeremiah can be sources of help for people to appropriately deal with any anger toward God that they experience.[30] Depression should be addressed with understanding and compassion while offering hope. Typically, depression is understood to be related to long term body chemistry but after a natural disaster anyone can be dealing with a sense

---

30. Lester, "Why Hast Thou Forsaken Me," 67.

The Psychological

of despondence or the "blues." Appropriate, measured, and authentic emotional transparency from you the preacher about how you have been helped through Scripture can help listeners see that the preached text has aided others.

Preaching calmly can aid those who are suffering with PTSD or ASD. Volume and inflexion should be moderate. This does not mean that passion cannot be present, but that it should be expressed with consideration of others emotional and/or mental states.

CHAPTER TWELVE

The Sociological

THE SURVIVORS OF A NED can be touched sociologically in both negative and positive aspects. The negative can be felt and experienced in numerous ways. As noted in Chapter Eleven, the culture of an area can be lost as an eventual result of a natural disaster. An entire way of life can be lost when the devastation wipes out industries and the means of livelihood or makes the locale uninhabitable. For many people their work or vocation is a significant arena for their social circles. No workplace or schoolroom can mean no time with friends or at least with other people.

Typical interaction within a family and among others in a community can be diminished if not lost all together, as well. Hopefully such diminishment is short-lived. But it is still experienced regardless of the duration. Normal patterns of interaction and healthy bonding rituals in relationships like family meals, birthday parties, holiday traditions, physical intimacy, and simple times of just being together can be disrupted. This disruption can contribute to strains on normally healthy relationships in marriage, family, the workplace, schools, churches, and among neighbors.

Relationships that are healthy before the disaster can be stretched and become troubled. Given the extreme conditions in which they may find themselves, people can act and react in ways they had not before. This affects others in a relationship with them as people see things about one another not previously noticed. Some behaviors, attitudes, conduct, and priorities may be entirely

The Sociological

new. For example, a formerly upbeat person may become depressed. Someone that was socially outgoing may become somewhat reclusive. Even physical injuries can alter the dynamics of a relationship. For some people these can essentially change the rules of engagement in the relationship.

As manufacturing stress tests reveal fractures in metal welds, so can the pressure, fatigue, and taxing experience of a natural disaster uncover previously unknown or unaddressed weaknesses in a relationship. Unfortunately, some weaknesses may make themselves known only at the moment of breakage. Just as natural disasters uncover inadequacies and flaws in organizations and governments,[1] they can have the same affect upon relationships. Marriages that were weak, family dysfunction that was crippling, suppressed relationship tensions, and relational issues long avoided can all be exposed and exploited by the event.

The Baton Rouge Flood of 2016 caused a housing shortage for the local population. Numerous individuals and families, friends and neighbors found it necessary to share housing both short-term and long-term. Living long-term in crowded quarters, whether with extended family or others, caused strain on relationships and created additional stress for individuals. Oft-repeated needs I heard in conversations were for privacy and personal space to completely relax.

But at the same time, there can be positive sociological affects from a natural disaster. The experience can strengthen bonds, increase solidarity, and enhance marital satisfaction.[2] The factors that make for positive or negative outcomes for family units is not yet fully understood,[3] however, as resiliency and robustness are factors for individuals' positive recovery it is logical to assume that these qualities can play a factor for families, too.

Communities and neighborhoods as a whole can be sociologically affected in a positive way. People very often help one another regardless of race, creed, lifestyle, or status. Help is extended to not

---

1. Taylor, *Disaster and Disaster Stress*, 38.
2. Tierney, "Social and Community Contexts," 30.
3. Tierney, "Social and Community Contexts," 31.

only friends and immediate neighbors but strangers. A disaster tends to level the field as all people are facing the same challenges, hurts, and kinds of needs. Old grievances can become insignificant and set aside as people come together in a common crisis. New friendships can form between old neighbors that had no interactions until helping one another through the crisis.

Coaching for Preaching

To prepare listeners for the worship service and for the sermon, incorporate opportunities and times for the congregation to socialize. From my experience, it is very unlikely that there will be time for typical small group meetings or all-church fellowships in people's schedules. Therefore, having coffee and breakfast pastries available and encouraging people to arrive earlier for worship services when they are able can create the space for socialization in people's lives. Our church did this many Sundays throughout our recovery and rebuild phases.

It was a special blessing to our congregation when a church from outside our area came and cooked Sunday lunch one weekend for Covenant Community Church. They brought and setup tables in our gutted, bare-floor sanctuary, cooked, and hand-served the meal. The delight, joy, and appreciation of our congregation was very evident! Like the spirituality of addressing practical needs, social interaction has a profound spiritual dimension, too.

Arrange for individual parishioners to share in a worship service with the congregation a story of God's faithfulness to them during the previous week. This can be done in a designated time in the service or incorporated into the sermon as an illustration of God's faithfulness. Both I and one of the other local pastors observed that doing this gave people a sense of needed connection with one another.

Be authentic and speak of the strain and tension that relationships can experience under the adversity of a NED. Unfortunately, people in close, long-term relationships likely have seen one another act in new or different ways than before. Do not step back from the subject of forgiveness—both the asking for and the giving of forgiveness. Preach about extending mercy and grace to others.

Remind born-again listeners of who they are in Christ. As people are absorbing new experiences about themselves and integrating that to reconstruct their view of themselves, it is important that they know their true identity in Christ. Assure them of Christ's acceptance of them; of his continual patient working with them for their Christlikeness.

Being physically present with one another in the presence of God is fundamental to being a church. During both the preparation and delivery of a sermon, the preacher should personally recognize that a congregation being under the proclamation of the Word of God together is, in itself, a bonding and belonging experience. The fellowship of the Holy Spirit in such settings is a spiritual reality that can be psychologically and socially renewing. Never doubt the working of the Holy Spirit in unseen, unaccounted ways.

CHAPTER THIRTEEN
The Spiritual

PSYCHOLOGISTS AND SOCIOLOGISTS RECOGNIZE that religious beliefs or spirituality have a benefit for individuals in their recovery from a NED. It also has a role in post-traumatic growth. This benefit comes from several factors. First, whatever religious belief system an individual may have, typical to them all is the tenet that there is a higher power and that the disaster with its resulting effects are from the goodness and will of this higher power. As Christians we know this higher power as the personal, triune God revealed in the Bible. Second, most religions involve participation in some form of faith-based community which lends support in life and especially during a disaster. Third, many forms of spirituality advocate a harmonious relationship with nature. Fourth, some religious perspectives hold that spirituality can be expressed as an abiding belief in oneself even during trying situations such as disasters.[1] In addition to these, the Christian preacher may observe that some who were previously not interested in spirituality or religion may begin to search for answers to existential questions. This presents a great opportunity for the gospel preacher.

But each of these factors can be challenged by a NED. Not only can the tenets of one's faith become questioned, but the tenets themselves may produce questions. What is the will of God (or one's higher power if that is their belief system)? Where is his benevolence? If

---

1. Zelinski, "Our Critical Issues" 173.

travel is not possible, how can one assemble with their faith-family? Believing in a harmonious relationship with nature, why has nature turned upon us? Why have I let myself and others down?

Christian pastors and preachers naturally recognize that people have daily spiritual needs. By definition, preaching addresses spiritual needs. But for many after a disaster, like in other areas of their lives, the survivors' spiritual needs may be different than they were before. That difference may be one of degrees rather than of kind, but it is still there. Doubts of God may arise even within the most pious. Questions of his involvement, his promises, and feelings of abandonment can grow into a spiritual crisis. The ages-long question of "Why?" can be repeated. Anger toward God may be experienced.

Weaknesses in personality or perceived character issues may emerge even among those who see themselves as spiritually mature. Disappointment with oneself can induce guilt. Over the course of an extended recovery and rebuilding phase the lack of physical rest can make a person grumpy, demanding, and just generally disagreeable. This can feed into one's disappointment with themself. Due to the demand of time and energy necessary to recover and rebuild as quickly as possible, the neglect of one's spiritual or devotional life can take a toll on one's spiritual wellbeing.

Coaching for Preaching

A helpful sermon application is to encourage the confession of one's shortcomings. Confession to God of one's failures is always appropriate. A believer may need to wisely make confession of their conduct or attitude to one or two mature believers. Certainly in order to reconcile with a person that one has offended, confession to that person needs to be done. Such sermon application should be accompanied with preaching of the promises of God's grace, forgiveness, and the promised presence of Christ as believers confess to one another (Matt 18:20).

SECTION THREE

Draw from Job's story and example to help people see that it is acceptable to humbly ask questions. Help listeners see that asking questions may not be an issue but the attitude and heart disposition of the inquirer can be. Not only is Job an example of this but so are many of the psalmists who wrote laments.

Related to the above, be honest that the problem of evil perplexes belief systems of any sort, Christianity included. While most theological systems attempt to answer questions about the reason for suffering and evil, I have observed that at times none of the answers seem fully to satisfy one's doubts. Your listeners need to hear that it is then that honestly admitting one's lack of understanding but still choosing to trust God may be the most courageous act of faith.

CHAPTER FOURTEEN

The Community

MANY OF THE EFFECTS of a NED upon an individual play out across the community at large. The physical destruction of terrain, infrastructure, facilities, and the stretching of limited resources can impact the function and personality of a community. As noted earlier, the very survival of a community can be called into question due to environmental damage or by the necessity of addressing possible future disasters. Community-wide questions of how rebuilding will affect neighborhoods, what will governmental powers require or demand, and who receives help and who does not, can begin to test the bonds within communities. Disruption of community services ranging from public utilities to support agencies can have both short-term and long-term affects upon a community.

Often people of a local community will gather at the anniversary of a disaster to receive and give support to one another. It is not unusual for these gatherings to be hosted or sponsored by churches. Local preachers are likely to be called upon to address the gathering, even if the occasion is not church sponsored. This possibility again underscores the importance of knowing the audience in order to effectively preach. Within the community there are particular groups toward which to be attentive.

SECTION THREE

VULNERABLE GROUPS

Some groups within the community are more vulnerable than others. Halpern and Tramontin notes that children, the elderly, those with mental health issues, as well as people with physical disabilities have unique challenges and needs in a natural disaster.[1] The homeless can be added to this list as well. Though a citizen may fit within one or more of these identified groups, the individual may or may not necessarily have the difficulties common within the group. Being aware of these possibly vulnerable groups does not imply that each individual requires unique or special care, as resiliency and functionality can vary by individual. Still, when you are preaching it is helpful to identify such groups and recognize their needs. They are blessed knowing that they are not being ignored or forgotten. And the church is blessed by being reminded that some among them and the community need special attention. This need is a great opportunity to serve others.

FIRST RESPONDERS/CIVIC LEADERS

A group easily overlooked within the community that is directly affected by a NED is that of first responders. These men and women who live within or near affected areas likely have been touched by the disaster personally. Yet their responsibility requires that they move past their own immediate needs and those of their family to help others. A similar but perhaps smaller group is that of civic officials that must manage the crisis for themselves and the community at large. In the ongoing rebuilding phase these officials often are subjected to the stress of making difficult decisions when there are no win-win solutions, navigating politically charged situations, being misunderstood by the public as well as the impact on their own personal lives. Your preaching ought to include this group and their needs.

---

1. Halpern and Tramontin, *Disaster Mental Health*, 137–170.

The Community

POSITIVE EFFECTS

It should be noted that not all effects of a NED upon a community are negative. Community challenges can be answered by heroic, selfless, and altruistic actions of individuals within the community. Volunteers emerge even from among the survivors themselves. Heroic figures can often be professional first responders or a stranger. Later, as stories are shared about such actions a community can be given a sense of appropriate pride about itself that such people live within the affected area. This positive effect and the stories of individuals that have exemplified them can be a great source for sermon illustrations.

Preaching considerations

Invitations to participate in large community gatherings and smaller community-based support groups should be readily accepted and prepared for prayerfully. Such meetings and groups will likely form after the disaster. If asked to preach at such an occasion, you should prepare a biblical message, preach with the voice of a pastor, and clearly announce that salvation, hope, and comfort are found in Jesus Christ. On such an occasion, it is possible, with careful, thorough, and prayerful preparation to uncompromisingly present the gospel with sensitivity to other religions and faiths. Sensitivity should also be directed toward the physical, psychological, financial, and social pain that many in attendance will be experiencing.

While preaching to either one's own congregation or to a community gathering, call people to be good neighbors by helping one another and serving the vulnerable groups within the community. This sermon application can cause

SECTION THREE

manifold blessings throughout the community at large. Remember that the people of God are moved by a Holy Spirit sparked instinct to help others even when they themselves are suffering. Often believers only need to be made aware of others and their needs.

Enlighten listeners to the needs of first responders and the challenge of being a civic leader during a crisis. Opportunity for frustration and anger directed toward civic leaders can abound. Preaching that does not scold listeners for their possible negative attitude toward others but rather encourages a disposition defined by the fruit of the Spirit is impactful upon the community.

CHAPTER FIFTEEN

The Church

LIKE INDIVIDUALS AND COMMUNITIES, local churches can also be physically, psychologically, socially, financially, and spiritually affected by a NED. As individuals respond according to personality, so do local churches respond according to corporate personality. Churches also take action during and after a NED according to their make-up of congregants. A church composed more of people with practical building skills may choose to be available to help a community with its buildings while a church composed more of managerial people may be more involved with coordinating the efforts of outside organizations and people. Churches have different resources within them and through their network or denomination. These can be not only factors for how a church responds to the needs of the community but how it addresses its own needs. One church may do the necessary repairs with volunteered skills and labor from within. Another may choose to hire a professional contractor to do the work and yet another may use both.

THE PHYSICAL

Physically destructive powers in a community are no respecter of persons or places—church facilities can be as damaged as any other. A place to gather for worship is an immediately recognizable need for a congregation after a NED. A congregation may not be able to

SECTION THREE

gather the first week after a disaster. But, if at all possible, a church needs to gather in some way by the second week. Local congregational life can be disrupted by a disaster in the same ways as family life. The same recovery and rebuilding challenges and frustrations that homeowners and local businesses face, congregations face, too.

THE PSYCHOLOGICAL

Psychologically churches are affected. I shared earlier the emotional response expressed in our first worship service after the Baton Rouge Flood. That was atypical of our congregation. A local pastor in the Baton Rouge Flood shared that his congregation had to make a transition in their mindset. Before the flood, the congregation was accustomed to providing help and aid to others in need. But now they were the ones in need of help. The same is true for the church I pastored through the flood. You and your congregation may have to navigate the humbling but blessed effect of being recipients of help and aide.

THE SOCIOLOGICAL

The impediments that a NED creates can cause local churches to lose their sense of connectedness within the congregation. Service schedules and frequency of meeting may be changed due to the demands of recovery and rebuilding. Individuals' opportunity to gather can be affected as well. Adequate facilities in which to meet may not be available. A healthy, thriving congregation that is warm and relational can, like a marriage, experience relationship strains due to lack of time together, difficult decisions that must be made together about the church and its future, and the fact that some people relocate both temporarily and permanently.

THE SPIRITUAL

Spiritually, a natural disaster can cause distraction from the unique mission and vision of a local church. It has been observed that as

The Church

suddenly as the disaster itself, a church's plans, preparations for those plans, and anticipated gains from those plans may have to be abandoned to deal with the immediate crisis. Over the course of recovery and rebuilding, the mission and vision of the local church can narrow to only restoring the lives of those around them. This is very understandable and is as it should be as changing priorities are forced upon the church.

But this change of priority also brings the danger of losing sight of essential evangelistic and discipling ministry. In fact, many if not most programmed ministries may have to be suspended due to lack of leaders and volunteers, no available time, and/or lack of funding. Throughout the recovery and rebuild of Covenant Community Church, I was concerned about becoming "a Sunday-service-only church."

One of the long-term spiritual effects of a NED that I have experienced is the challenge of reestablishing long-time suspended ministries. A disaster is an event that can cause a church to reevaluate its purpose and priorities. That can be a positive as it is an opportunity to prayerfully make needed changes in direction or vision. Negatively, however, people lose good spiritual disciplines such as serving and faithful attendance in public worship. In short, the rhythm of life for the local church can be affected and can be difficult to reestablish.

FINANCIAL AFFECTS

Previously unmentioned for individuals and communities but just as real for them and for churches is the financial impact of a NED. Several factors mitigate the financial effect upon each—income levels, having insurance or not, the degree of destruction to property, and the effect upon congregants' employment.[1] Individual and business income, tax revenue for government, and contributions for churches can all be affected.

---

1. Flood insurance is a separate insurance for homes, businesses, and churches that typically is not carried unless located in a flood plain and/or required by a mortgage company.

SECTION THREE

The churches in Central, Louisiana whose facilities flooded faced huge financial challenges. Those whose facilities did not flood were still affected financially due to the number of members that flooded. The Christian impulse to help those in need can still motivate churches in attempts to provide aid to the community as well as to other churches. But this generosity potentially strains church finances even more.

Coaching for Preaching

Immediately secure and announce a place for the congregation to gather for worship and for hearing the Word of God. This likely will be a time for creativity. Solutions can be as different as each church. Perhaps an auxiliary building on the church property can be used. Churches can coordinate their schedules and share facilities. Going exclusively online is an option and can be extremely helpful for the church whose members become temporarily displaced and scattered even across the nation. The search for an ideal meeting solution is likely futile. Expect to make trade-offs that will have to be done in order to meet.

Preach about God's faithfulness as a provider. This helps both churches and individuals. To encourage Covenant Community Church, I would highlight for the congregation gifts and offerings sent to the church from any outside sources. While our ushers were receiving tithes and offerings in our services, I would announce outside gifts and offerings received during the week which were being included that Sunday. I would tell the amount and which outside group sent it. As the congregation applauded with thanks to God, it became noticeable that this supported the

The Church

preaching of God's faithfulness with nearly weekly tangible illustrations of his character.

Remind the church in sermons that the crisis is temporary, but that God's purpose for that local congregation is still in place. On occasion, review the local church's vision and mission while still recovering and rebuilding. This need not be done as a rally cry but as a gentle encouragement to look beyond the immediate crisis toward a bright future.

CHAPTER SIXTEEN

Further Coaching for Addressing Listener's Needs

You may be looking at the same faces following a NED in your locale, but you are not preaching to the same people. Especially in the immediate aftermath of all that has happened. They are a tired people, a distressed people, a confused people. Some have had traumatic losses. For many of them this will not be over by the end of the week. Recovery can last for months. Rebuilding can last for years. But God's Word is unchangeable, and while you are experiencing much of all the same, people need to hear from God's Word through you.

Encourage resilience and robustness. In an email response to my question "What would you suggest pastors say to their congregations in a sermon(s) after a natural environmental disaster?" neuropsychologist Darlene Nemeth wrote, "In this hour of need, we must be resilient." While resilience and robustness can be innately present or absent from people, the preacher can present biblical truth that 1) inflames these innate qualities or 2) is used by the Holy Spirit to impart such qualities to those who need them. As Aten and Broan noted that resiliency can be developed,[1] preaching can be a tool that the Holy Spirit uses to grow this in a listener.

The life stories of Joseph and Job can be texts used to inspire listeners to be resilient. Other possibilities include texts from the

---

1. Aten and Broan, *Spiritual First Aid*, 11.

Further Coaching for Addressing Listener's Needs

life of Moses, David, and Jeremiah as each not only survived but eventually thrived through their ordeal. God's promises of strength, of his coming to the aide of the weak and weary, and of his enabling people to be overcomers are excellent preaching themes that can impart resiliency and robustness to survivors.

Preach God's goodness. This is other than repeating a mantra to convince people who are facing a reality that insinuates otherwise about God. Preaching God's goodness that ministers to the survivors of a disaster draws directly from biblical texts. It also is illustrated by the stories and providential happenings in the lives of people within the disaster. As stated earlier, I view the book of Job as revealing an appropriate response of the righteous when suffering. One can "bless" or "curse" God. Choosing to bless God in suffering enables one to see his goodness. It continues to be true that not everything that happens is good, but God does work for the good of those who are his. For some specific situations, the preacher may need to lovingly, gently, and patiently present the truth that because God is good, he is acting on an eternal purpose in temporal disasters.

Preach honestly. Regardless of one's theological views within orthodox Christianity, questions about suffering and evil are very difficult. Like me, you may find it challenging to answer every question to anyone's satisfaction—perhaps even your own. But it is allowable and in many cases wise to say, "I don't know the answer to that." It is equally wise to remind people that God can be trusted with mystery. We may not know everything; but what we do know of God is that he is trustworthy. To choose to trust God in the midst of one's suffering, loss, and pain is a great act of faith.

Preach comfort.[2] Directly or indirectly through extended families and their circle of friends, many people will be dealing to some degree with some type of loss. Not every sermon should be a funeral sermon, but the residual pain of loss will be persistent for your listeners. Consider a sermon or a brief series of sermons about grief and loss. If a series of consecutive grief sermons

---

2. While the following three preaching coaching points were independently derived from my own observations, they are confirmed by Jamie Aten of the Humanitarian Disaster Institute. Aten, "Preaching in the Wake of Disaster."

seems inappropriate for the congregation but one sermon seems inadequate, then occasionally address the subject through sermon application.

Preach hope. The preaching of hope is always appropriate in any situation but especially so in the aftermath of a natural disaster. Psychological research consistently tells of the role that hope plays in the emotional and/or mental well-being of people.

It is documented that disasters uncover inadequacies and flaws in organizations and governments.[3] The preacher should be aware that this is also the case for individuals, family systems, and local churches. The wise preacher ministering within the context of a NED will recognize that his listeners are struggling with these revelations and the influence of flaws and inadequacies. Proclaiming the truth of good news within the gospel that reveals God's rescuing of flawed and inadequate people bolsters listeners' hope. It also is the means whereby the Holy Spirit prompts his fruit of patience in relationships and with situations.

Preach community. Spiritual isolation, while not necessarily an intentional choice, can happen due to workload demand in both the short-term and long-term in the aftermath of a disaster. Occasionally, remind your listeners to be aware of this danger. Community can be implied by the use of the first personal plural while preaching. Speaking of "us" and "we" can help listeners recognize that they are not alone.

While preaching fulfills its same role for the community of listeners as before the disaster, afterward it can also be a psychological comfort by being a familiar ritual in which the listener participates. Consider adjusting the elements of weekly worship services and their length to provide opportunity for people to live the community that you are preaching. Sometimes sermon application may be to take the last 15 minutes of the service time and allow individuals to share their situation with the person beside them and then pray together.

Preach the gospel. While preaching to comfort, encourage, console, and to enlighten listeners, the preacher should also preach

---

3. Taylor, *Disaster and Disaster Stress*, 38.

Further Coaching for Addressing Listener's Needs

to evangelize. A disaster presents opportunities to address the deepest questions, longings, and emptiness of humanity. Just as people's needs are different after the crisis, people's openness to the gospel can be different after the crisis.

Each of these considerations can also be sermon applications. Your listeners can be equipped and encouraged to share Christ as you make them aware of the opportunity the natural disaster creates. Your church's influence in the community can continue even if organized ministries are shut down to focus on recovery. That influence can be through your listeners offering hope and comfort to fellow survivors. Or, through the telling to others of their story of God's goodness. While these are acts believers should be regularly doing in any circumstance, your preaching can inspire and remind them during all the distractions and demands of recovery and rebuilding after a NED.

SECTION FOUR

Faithful Preaching in a Natural Environmental Disaster, Or: "Preach it!"

Is THERE ONE THING and one thing only that a preacher, a pastor must do when life has been shaken, blown away, flooded, scorched, struck? When so much of one's life, one's community, one's church and ministry has been literally turned upside down is there some action that one can focus upon? If a to-do list cannot be formed because so many changes happen by the time it is written, is there one thing that must be done each day? What is the one necessity that binds together everything else that disaster recovery and rebuilding requires of a preacher? What brings clarity for a preacher's life and service amidst the chaos caused by a NED? The answer is laid out in two words—be faithful!

This is a trait seen in all the principal individuals whose lives were part of the five biblical NEDs presented earlier. Noah was faithful to obey God's instructions both prior to and during the flood of Genesis. Joseph remained faithful to God throughout his entire sojourn in Egypt. Job, though perplexed and pained, endured faithful to God in his suffering. Joel faithfully proclaimed God's

SECTION FOUR

message to ancient Israel. The early church was faithful to serve in the Jerusalem Famine. From these five examples the following definition for faithfulness as a preacher in a NED can be derived: *Being faithful as a preacher in a NED is loyally obeying God through the complexities and perplexities of the event while continuing to preach the Word of God and serving others' practical needs.*

When a preacher or pastor experiences a NED in their locale, one can be an effective preacher by being faithful about the event itself, faithful among the survivors of the event, faithful in one's calling, and faithful to God. These four areas are distinct from one another but are not distant from one another. They can and often do intersect with one another.

CHAPTER SEVENTEEN
Faithful About the Event

AS ONE WOULD EXPECT, it was difficult preaching the first Sunday we worshiped together after the flood destroyed and damaged so much. It was one week after the event. The week was like one long one hundred and sixty-eight-hour day punctuated by short pauses for naps. It was well into the week before I could find a quit place to prepare for preaching that Sunday. It was nearly last minute by my routine before I found the time to prepare. Usually, I prepare sermons one week ahead. But the sermon prepared for that Sunday no longer seemed relevant if I may say that without it being misunderstood that God's Word (not mine) is ever irrelevant.

The flood was bigger than any eight-hundred-pound gorilla in a room. How do you ignore something of that magnitude? Is it possible to do so? Is it wise to do so?

Well, "having been there and done that" along with the research from this project, I say the answers to these three questions are, in order, "You can't," "No," and "No." In fact, it is wisest to speak to people directly of the event. It is on everyone's mind. It comes up in nearly every conversation. For some people it likely sneaks into their dreams at night.

Something significant has happened in your community and to you, your family, and your church—you have been struck by a natural environmental disaster. Regardless of its form or the degree of impact, to meet and overcome it one must face it as the reality that it is. What is true of any challenge one faces as a leader is true of preaching in a NED—a leader has a powerful role in defining the situation. And the best way to do that in a natural disaster is by being faithful about the event itself. There are at least five practical ways to be faithful about the event.

The first way is to *directly address the event in the first sermon preached after the NED*. This is the time for one's sermon theme to be fully built around the local NED. The full impact of the NED will likely not be known within the first week, but the freshness of the listeners' woundedness calls for comfort, soothing, and reassurance from God's Word. As with all sermons, it is essential for the sermon to be derived from, informed, and shaped by a biblical text. The text must not be overshadowed by the event. However, the NED can provide the sermon introduction, applications, and illustrations of the text. After the first sermon and then throughout the recovery and rebuilding process, use your own personal judgment to measure how often to refer to the NED in a sermon.

Over the weeks and months that follow, you can address the effects of a NED without invoking the NED itself. The physical, psychological, social, and spiritual needs that are present after the NED can be tackled from the pulpit without anchoring their cause to the NED. They can be spoken of simply as the needs that they are.

A second way to be faithful about the event is *not to insist that what has happened is a divine message of judgment upon the community*. Be humble enough to accept that one does not know with biblical certainty that the event is a specific divine message. Whatever your personal conviction about the possible meaning of the disaster, judgment must be formed with professional decorum and out of pastoral care. This decision should be made through the framework of the Bible and solid theology, not from personal impressions. If one's theology allows for impressions prompted by the Holy Spirit, remember that as such they are to be measured by the Bible.

Be understanding that assigning judgment is not helpful in the immediate aftermath of a NED. People need hope, strength, and comfort. Listeners can be called to evaluate their lives according to God's righteousness, to reflect upon their lives, to evaluate their lifestyles, and to repentance without assigning a meaning of judgment to the NED. While it is human nature to seek out meaning, it is wiser for the preacher to direct people's thoughts toward an explanation such as creation's groaning for the revealing of the sons of God (Rom 8:22) rather than as an act of divine judgment.

A third way to be faithful about the event is a follow-up to the second—*share with listeners that what has happened can be thought of as a test and/or a challenge to them and their faith.* This is your influence as a leader defining the reality of what has happened. A NED is challenging in many ways to everyone whether they are born again or not, and anyone may question God's character. A Christ follower in a way not previously, can be tested in their relationship with God as they are now in a situation with which they must trust God, remain faithful to him, and/or feel overwhelmingly discouraged. Addressing this directly from the pulpit is genuine pastoral preaching. The preacher who does so can be commended for caring for people's souls during the challenging time.

Be faithful to preach sermons that equip and empower your listeners to meet the challenge or test. It is not enough to frame the event and offer perspective. Preach about overcoming challenges as you would any other time but now identify the challenges specifically and concretely—the natural disaster and its affects.

Reminding listeners that God created the physical laws that cause NED is a fourth way to be faithful about the event as a preacher. The natural forces and dynamics of weather and the environment were created as good by God's critique. They conformed to his specifications when created. But now, those laws and dynamics are marred and conflicted as a consequence of humanity's sin. The world that God deemed as good is now broken. What has happened in the natural environmental disaster that you and your community have experienced is a consequence of this brokenness.

Faithfully reminding your listeners of this truth can help them avoid the despair of living in a world that they see as entirely accidental. Your preaching can help people overcome potential depression or worsening depression as you declare the truth that the universe has not formed itself as an evil, dangerous place. Rather, it is a lovingly created but broken place in which God has intervened to begin restoring it through Jesus Christ. The recovery and

SECTION FOUR

rebuilding of creation is yet to be completed by God, but it will surely be completed by him.

This next way to be faithful about the event seems counterintuitive. Everyone is trying to move past what has happened in their lives. It would seem wise to not mention it any more than one must. But it should be mentioned. Therefore, a fifth way to be faithful about the event is to *mark the first anniversary of the event*. This is both customary and healthy. This intersects with being faithful among the survivors as in all likelihood their thoughts are upon what happened one year ago. As observed previously, the first anniversary can be acknowledged by preaching a sermon that relates God's faithfulness, reviews accomplishments of the church and the community since the disaster, and encourages people to be thankful and loyal to God.

Marking the first anniversary in a sermon gives people a sense of permission to talk about what they are feeling. Speaking of underlying emotions can establish a benchmark where they can realize how much they have emotionally progressed, or, how they are still being affected. As a preacher you may feel similar to the way a friend feels about not want to bring up memories of another friend's deceased loved one. But as you have probably learned the friend is already thinking of the lost loved one and is heartened by knowing that others have not forgotten their deceased parent, spouse, child, or special person. Marking the anniversary can have the same positive uplift.

CHAPTER EIGHTEEN
Faithful Among the Survivors

A PARISHIONER OF PASTOR Brown's was hit with a triple whammy. The church member was served with divorce papers from his wife. He was becoming another story of family failure. What would this mean for his future? The future of his children? Was he to think about the future of his wife now? His life was filled with all of these questions and emotions too entangled to quickly sort.

The next day after receiving papers for divorce, the Baton Rouge Flood filled the man's house with water. Not only was his home being devastated but the building that represented the once happy home was now devastated. What a picture of his life in that moment!

With a Job-like irony, as the man was processing the divorce and working to restore the house, he needed surgery. What else was going to happen? Could he carry any more burdens? Isn't enough, enough?!

While his church was being the base for his denomination's relief efforts in the area, coordinating help to the flooded families in his own church, fulfilling the ongoing pastoral administrative duties and those of the pulpit, Pastor Brown stayed close to the man as his world collapsed. Brown was in continual touch, offering help to cheer the man, keeping him motivated to persevere through all the hardship as he was likely most affected by the disaster of the flood.

Pastor Brown was being faithful among the survivors.

SECTION FOUR

The Old Testament prophet Ezekiel's life and ministry were unique—as can be said about most preachers. But his was a truly different time and setting. He, along with thousands of other Israelites, were exiled in Babylon by divine action. After much warning to his people, God enacted his discipline upon them. Babylon was used to carry away the majority of the people of God from the land, the home, the place he had promised them.

Ezekiel's book of recorded revelations and prophecies opens with him "among the exiles by the Chebar canal" (Ezek 1:1). As God's man, he was living the same exiled experience as those to whom he was sent (Ezek 3:11). It was among the exiles that Ezekiel had his first recorded encounter with the glory of God in a vision. And, it was through this overwhelming encounter that Ezekiel was called as a prophet sent to God's people (Ezek 2:3–5). His ministry as a prophet not only commenced but culminated "among the exiles."

You see the point for yourself. God calls people to serve "among" others. And like Ezekiel, being "among" others can entail living the experiences that others live. Preaching in the aftermath of a NED is most often done by preachers who are "among" the survivors of the disaster. Not only has one lived many of the same experiences, but one should see themselves as called to be in the midst of the crisis and its aftermath. And like any other time or context of ministry, the preacher is to be faithful—faithful among the survivors.

I have identified ten tactics available to us as preachers for being faithful among the survivors beginning with *intentionally seeking out interaction with them*. The conversations one has with people who experienced a disaster will likely be one-sided. Actively listening to people relate their experiences is a great emotional and psychological help to survivors. These conversations can occur naturally in the course of a day as one is going about their own work of recovery and rebuilding.

While these conversations can occur naturally they may not be automatic. If noticing that such interaction is not happening, then aggressively be intentional to connect with survivors. Visit people in or at their homes, walk slowly among those gathered for worship to be more approachable, listen to strangers tell their stories while shopping for your own supplies. Be curious about the progress families are making in rebuilding, learn what is frustrating them the most, celebrate each step toward recovery regardless of how small.

Like a novelist observing people and the activities around them to soak up details for a story, your attention to others will not only help people feel cared about but will give you understanding of those to whom you may preach. You can gain insights for sermon themes and practical application. Allow these conversations and interaction with others to influence your preaching. It is wisest not to give names when recounting others' stories unless you have permission to do so. But to appropriately relate someone's experience makes a sermon appealing to survivors as well as makes the sermon more clear like an excellent, well-placed illustration does.

While listening, utilize the second tactic for being faithful among the survivors—*be aware that individuals respond differently to a NED*. Among the many ways these differences can be accounted for are personality, life-experience, available resources, and/or the severity of one's situation. Some people are more resilient and robust than others. Everyone has a different social support system. One's sense of financial security can significantly affect how one responds to the crisis. Very simply, the degree of impact that the same local disaster had will vary even among next door neighbors.

Spiritually, people respond according to the spiritual direction of their lives and the drawing work of the Holy Spirit. As one pastor interviewed while researching this book stated, "Those who were moving toward God before the disaster continued to do so. Those moving away from God before the disaster continued to do so." This does not negate the Holy Spirit using the crisis to awaken someone spiritually, but that person will still respond differently than another person.

The third tactic is very important for effective pulpit ministry. It is to *make sermon application highly relevant to the immediate and long-term NED-related needs of the survivors.* When doing so you will be preaching directly about people's needs. This helps them in the immediate but also helps them see overall the relevance of the Bible to their daily lives.

SECTION FOUR

Some suggested disaster-related sermon applications include:

- Advocate planning and preparing for the future as did Joseph when warned about the famine.
- Encourage listeners to look for God's *hesed*. (See Chapter Six.) This affects the outlook and attitude of survivors by helping them to be optimistic, overcoming of despondency, and exalting of God in the midst of their situation.
- Address emotions such as grief, sorrow, anxiety and fear, anger, and depression by preaching comfort and hope.
- Offer biblical principles to navigate relationship issues that may have arisen out of the disaster.
- Lead listeners into confession both to God and appropriately to another of their failings and shortcomings throughout the process of recovery and rebuilding.
- Teach practical meanings of the born-again believer's identity in Christ.
- Encourage honest questions before God by showing how to ask the hard questions that arise from suffering and a natural disaster.
- Preach to call survivors to help one another and provide for others' practical needs when it is within one's own ability and resources. More than mirroring the actions of the Early Church's response to the Jerusalem Famine, preach how practical help is to be understood on par with spiritual help. It is as needed as prayer and counseling. Encourage listeners to be attentive to the often-overlooked needs of vulnerable groups, first responders, and civic leaders.
- Speak to relief workers that may be present in worship services. This includes both official and unofficial relief workers who have unique needs as relief workers. This group of people are easily overlooked and can feel taken for granted in a crisis. Some of them have put their lives and personal recovery on hold to help others.

Faithful Among the Survivors

A powerful tactic for faithfulness among the survivors is to *preach to lift needless guilt of those who have questions and negative emotions*. Job's example reveals that a righteous person can ask sincere questions, struggle with accepting events, and experience negative emotions while still remaining faithful to God. Anxiety, fear, and anger appear in the imprecatory Psalms as well as the laments of Jeremiah to name a few texts. Preach from these biblical texts.

Job's experience and the words of the psalmists can assure people that, like them, others before have struggled with confusion, anger, doubt, questions, and pain both in and about life. Preaching these texts assures listeners that having such doubts, questions, or emotions does not mean that one has lost their salvation. They can see from the inspired record of other faithful people that an understanding God can be approached honestly but reverentially. To secure people in their relationship with God, the Holy Spirit can use preaching that proclaims approaching God in humble honesty as a means of how faithful people deal with their negative experiences and emotions. This is very practical preaching that buttresses the emotional and mental health of listeners.

A fifth tactic that listeners will appreciate of the preacher being faithful among the survivors is *remembering that people are tired and can be distracted*. People may struggle being attentive and responsive to preaching due to fatigue and stress. Be accepting of this and adjust your expectations accordingly. Shorter sermons communicated in simpler terms can be more effective right now. Other elements of the worship service may also be adjusted in length as well.

At the same time, be aware that listeners' fatigue intersects with being faithful in one's calling, too. Sermons should not be reduced to only devotional thoughts. The worship service should not be diminished to a mere quiet time. During the crisis, people need the power of the Word of God. They especially need an awareness of Christ's presence in their lives which can be affirmed through worship.

The sixth tactic is preaching to *reassure and build faith*. People need reassurance after the trauma of a NED. They have been shocked by the event. Very tragically, some have lost people that they deeply love. It is possible that some have lost all the possessions they have accumulated over their lifetime. A preacher who is faithful among the survivors will, among other truths, declare God's love and his goodness. One will preach of the strength that comes from God and his restorative power. A faithful preacher will announce God's eagerness to forgive the repentant.

As the survivors' world is likely unfamiliar to them now, they may be disoriented by the events and their ramifications. Preaching the truth of God's eternality and faithfulness reassures listeners. Faithfully proclaiming God's promises and his character as a promise keeper builds the faith of people.

The seventh tactic for being faithful to the survivors in their situation is *preach with a calm spirit and tone of voice*. Some listeners may be dealing with PTSD or ASD. The preacher's volume and demeanor, while not needing to be passionless, can be calming to those listeners. Voice tone, word choice, body language, and overall mannerism in the pulpit should be very pastoral. Speak from the posture of being a non-anxious presence among the people.

An eighth tactic for faithfulness among the survivors is to *assure listeners that God cares for creation*. It is possible that crops, pets and/or livestock (which in some locales and situations can be economic wealth) have been affected if not lost in the NED. People often have an affinity with the fauna and flora of their locale and can feel a sense of its loss. A child's favorite climbing tree can be blown down. River courses can be altered by an earthquake literally moving a residence away from the water activities a family once enjoyed or depended upon for income. Pets can be lost.

Noah's story provides a foundation for one to understand that God cares about all of his creation, not only his human creation. He is aware of the sparrow and the flower of the field. To remember that God is faithful to provide for his creation and his people helps strengthen the attachment of survivors' faith in God. These enable and empower them to trust him as they work to recover their losses both economic and emotional.

Another highly effective tactic for being faithful among the survivors as a preacher is to *preach messages to stimulate resilience and robustness in the lives of the listeners*. Resilience, as defined earlier, is the ability to be firmly grounded in today while benefiting from yesterday so that one can see themselves in tomorrow. Robustness is simply strength and/or vigor that empowers people to deal with their situation.

Biblical texts and sermon themes that inspire, motivate, build faith, and inflame hope can be used by the Holy Spirit to both instill and encourage these qualities in listeners. Such texts include Abraham's and Sarah's long wait for a promised child, Naomi's sorrows and Ruth's losses turning into blessing, childless Hannah's personal pain becoming an act of dedicating a child to the Lord, and of course, Job. Apostle Paul's determination to spread the gospel, Stephen's unchanging witness to the point of death, and exiled Apostle John's being in the Spirit on the Lord's Day are all divinely inspired records that can cultivate personal resilience and robustness through God's strength.

The tenth tactic I offer for faithfulness among the survivors is to *preach and practice community*. People's lives can be incredibly filled with the demanding tasks of recovery and rebuilding. Relationships can become neglected, a sense of isolation can occur, or some people can simply withdraw from others. Such isolation is unhealthy in any circumstance.

The biblical metaphors of the Church as a body and a family can serve as sermon imagery that calls people into healthy community. More than a sermon about community is needed for community to be experienced. For an occasional application of a sermon on this theme consider adjusting the elements of the worship service to allow time for extended praying for one another and for socializing. Sermons about anger, forgiveness, and even communication skills are appropriate to promote community as well as tending strained relationships.

CHAPTER NINETEEN

Faithful in One's Calling

"I went into the pulpit tired, weary, worn out, a thousand things on my mind, but by God's grace I just acknowledge that I feel like the Lord used me during that time to speak to the people . . .. On one hand I guess they were more distracted, and they were more tired, and they could not sit still. But on the other hand, I mean their hearts were fertile ground."

Pastor Clark's description given in my interview with him provides a good summation of preaching in a NED. You have emotional, mental, and physical fatigue. Your worklist seems never-ending. And you face a gathering of people to preach to who are in the same situation as you. But the call of God still rests upon you. It motivates you to push through the fatigue with a strength you recognize as given to you by the Holy Spirit. And you are favored with moments of knowing that your labor is not in vain.

One who is called to preach is called to be faithful in service to God in two categories. One is serving his Word while the other is serving his people. This is true whether one is preaching in the aftermath of a NED or not. My personal experience and that of others interviewed in researching this book is that the pressures of being faithful in one's calling can understandably increase after a NED. One can feel paralyzed by the situation. This paralysis can come from two angles. One is having so much to do that one doesn't know what to do first and therefore does nothing. The other is that this is so unique of a situation, one's paralysis can be rooted in not knowing what to do so that one does nothing at all. A lack of training for dealing with such situations can contribute to one becoming significantly slowed if not stopped in their ministering to others and ministering from the pulpit.

There are several elements to being faithful in one's calling while dealing with the aftermath of a NED. These elements can be explored in the two categories mentioned above—faithful in the calling to people and faithful in the calling to God's Word. Faithfulness in one's calling to people in a NED has similarities with one's calling to people in general. There are some distinctions, however, if not in kind than certainly in degree.

The first element of being faithful in one's calling to people after a NED is *acknowledging and addressing both the practical and spiritual needs of people.* During the first week after a NED, the most practical need for a congregation is a place to worship. Secure a place and announce where the congregation will meet for gatherings if the church's facilities have been damaged. Remember that according to research, "place" is important for people. Gathering together is an act of worship and a congregation needs somewhere to do that.

On a more personal level, be active in helping people with their practical needs. Laboring alongside them in the toil of recovery and rebuilding has dividends for the pulpit. On Sunday, people seem to be more inclined to listen to someone who has sweated and strained alongside them during the week. This is truly being incarnational in ministry.

For the preacher that acknowledges the natural human need to be in community with others, being faithful in one's calling intersects with being faithful among the survivors. Consider allowing time in church gatherings for parishioners to share their stories, testimonies, or even where to find supplies. Some pastors find it easier to prioritize the spiritual over the physical or vice versa. But one's calling is to both, especially after a natural disaster.

Second, there is the element of *reminding people that they are not forgotten.* Delays in the arrival of help, lack of news coverage, prolonged response times, or having a very limited network of friends in the immediate vicinity are just some of the reasons that

SECTION FOUR

people may feel forgotten or unimportant in a NED. Unfortunately, some may actually be forgotten. The preacher can be faithful in his calling to people by reminding them in both conversations and from the pulpit that just as Noah, his family, and the animals on the ark were remembered by God, so are they as his people.

The pastoral needs of a congregation are not suspended by a NED—they continue as before. The pastor/preacher's attentiveness or that of other church leaders toward individuals in the church and community lets people know they have not been forgotten. A preacher is fortunate when one is part of a team of staff pastors or volunteers that can share this responsibility among themselves. People who feel remembered during the week can be more receptive to preaching on Sunday.

To be faithful in your calling to people, include the element of *reminding the local congregation that the crisis is temporary and that God's purpose for that congregation is still in place*. It is the preacher's calling to show how God's purposes as revealed in the Bible are to be fulfilled by the vision of a local church. This responsibility is still in place while recovering and rebuilding. A congregation can experience demographic, leadership, location, and financial changes in the aftermath of a NED. It is not only to God's glory but also for the health of the local congregation that sermons declare the truth that God's purpose still stands.

The second category to being faithful in one's calling is one's faithfulness to God's Word in a NED. As is the case with one's calling to people, one's calling to God's Word has similarities with typical preaching duties but again with distinctions in degree if not in kind. Therefore, the first and foremost element is—*preach*! Preach *honestly* when addressing people's needs and questions. Admit that questions about suffering and evil are difficult, but God can still be trusted when explanations are enigmatic. Preach *with confidence* in God, his Word, and his calling upon you. When preparing and preaching sermons, do so knowing that God is for you, his preacher. He continues to empower, enable, support, and provide for his preacher. Preach God's Word *with compassion*. Listeners need the reality of Jesus Christ who saw the crowds with compassion for they were harassed and helpless (Matt 9:36).

Faithful in One's Calling

Your faithfulness to God's Word is shown by you personally when in your own life there is the element of *trusting its power to positively affect people as it is preached*. God's Word is not altered, annulled, or in any way affected by a NED. It is eternally the same. As a preacher, trust that God's Word will be the lamp and light that people need to recover and rebuild their lives after a NED (Ps 119:105). Without a personal faith in the Bible as God's Word, one will be reluctant to preach it with confidence. That can undermine its potential influence upon people. The preacher's trust in God's Word does not assure that the listener will also trust in God's Word. But how can someone listen to one who does not believe the veracity of their own message? The preacher's own conviction of the power of God's Word at the least gives an example that people need.

To be faithful to the Word of God in one's calling *practice healthy self-care to be at one's best within the circumstances*. A preacher is not exempt from the demands and fatigue that comes with recovering and rebuilding after a NED. One must physically and mentally rest at regular intervals. If possible, utilize other preachers to take an occasional break from the pulpit. Local retired preachers may be happy to help carry some of the load.

If you are a retired preacher, consider making yourself available to local pastors in your area. Whether ministering in another's pulpit to ease some of the burden or helping with pastoral counseling, visitation, or administration one can offer immeasurably valuable service. Be aware that in whatever role, one may need to serve voluntarily as the church may be under heavy financial strain and unable to provide an honorarium.

It is very possible that the demands and circumstances of one's situation may be such that one is overtaxed physically, mentally, and spiritually regardless of one's pacing or prioritizing. If that is your situation, act as responsibly as possible and expect God to do what one cannot do. It is one thing to ignore presumptuously the command of a sabbath rest and another to be overwhelmed by no opportunity to rest.

Consider the concrete advice concerning self-care offered from pastors who have experienced preaching in a natural environmental disaster:

- Be alert to the effects of long-term adrenaline production and how you are responding to it. Common indicators of long-term adrenaline production can include muscle tension, headaches, shortness of breath, intestinal discomfort, heartburn, decreased libido, and changes in menstruation.[1] Monitor yourself by these as gauges on your dashboard.
- Seek out and be receptive to the advice from others that have experienced a NED.
- To encourage having a healthy attitude, do something daily that contributes to recovering or rebuilding regardless of how small that action may be.
- Eat healthfully, get sleep, and exercise regularly to relieve stress. Hopefully, these are habits that you have been practicing long before a NED.

Your faithfulness to God's Word as a preacher is publicly displayed by preaching. The fundamentals of homiletics still apply when preaching after a NED. But emphasis may need to be placed on the following:

- Continue the fundamentals of solid sermon preparation and delivery. An allowance may be made for developing shortcuts that are only effective during the crisis. But prayer, the discovery of the exegetical idea of a text, the development of a theme or big idea for the sermon from the text, organizing the sermon, illustrating, and application are non-negotiable fundamentals.
- Stay text-driven in one's preaching. The NED can be a sermon theme while also providing application and illustration, but a biblical text should always define and shape the sermon.
- Establish a location dedicated to sermon preparation. This is another expression of the role that "place" plays in people's lives. This helps a preacher retreat from the demands of recovery and rebuilding to focus on the sermon. The location need not be ideal, it only needs to be available.

1. American Psychological Association, "Stress Effects on the Body."

- Rather than planning sermons on a timeframe, do so according to threshold moments—events which signal a transition into another phase of recovery for your congregation. Also, anticipate the stages of psychological recovery presented in Chapter Eleven and address these. My practice of continual consecutive exposition allowed me to have a plan for preaching but to make application of the text according to needs of the listeners and changing situations. This gave me a framework for preaching so as not to start entirely from scratch each week, but it also gave me much flexibility to address the ever-changing needs of people.
- Make necessary adjustments in the moment of preaching to be effective. Allow yourself the freedom to be more extemporaneous if you usually are not. I am not advocating a lack of preparation but urging a conscious dependence on the Holy Spirit while in the pulpit.

Another element of your faithfulness to God's Word is to *prayerfully accept and then prepare for possible invitations to participate in larger community gatherings and smaller support groups.* Meetings like these are not uncommon after a NED or other community crisis. If you are extended such an invitation, recognize it as an opportunity to share and apply God's Word to the lives of people that you may not ever preach to on a Sunday. An opportunity like this is not a moment for an attitude of being "platformed" and gaining personal notoriety. Rather it is an opportunity for God's Word to be "platformed" and to be given notoriety among some who may not have given it any true consideration before. Accept invitations to speak in these venues without ego but with much eagerness to spread God's Word in the community.

The last and most important element of faithfulness to God's Word is *preaching the gospel.* This is paramount in faithfulness to God's Word. As noted earlier, people's lives move in different spiritual directions and the Holy Spirit draws people to Christ. As you know, it is through the preaching of the gospel that people come to faith in Jesus Christ and experience life transformation. This is an element of faithfulness that should always be present in our

SECTION FOUR

preaching, but as stated about faithfulness to serve people, it is the degree that is different not the kind. The aftermath of a NED can offer greater degrees of opportunity for people to come to Christ through the truth of the gospel in your sermons.

CHAPTER TWENTY
Faithful to God

PASTOR TOM SAT WITH me to share his experiences of being personally flooded and preaching to his congregation for the many months that the people of his congregation recovered and rebuilt. Being bi-vocational, Pastor Tom also had the responsibilities of leading a significant NGO in the community. As we sat and he related his experiences the subject of personal devotion and prayer became part of the conversation. In transparent honesty and through teary eyes, he admitted with personal disappointment that for the first time in his ministry, his responsibilities were so overwhelming that his prayer life waned. Restoring his devotional life outside of sermon preparation became a priority for his personal spiritual health. But it was also a priority as an expression of his being faithful to God .

This vignette from Pastor Tom's story is about a necessity for a preacher in a natural environmental disaster—faithfulness to God. Faithfulness to God is key to being fruitful in all circumstances and especially so when preaching after a natural disaster. Yet, being faithful to God can be a multifaceted challenge to which one must rise. I suggest that you consider three priorities that will aide you in maintaining your faithfulness to God in the demands you experience after a NED. Each of these priorities are equal in significance, but I will number them as we go.

The first priority is your *personal devotion to God*. Be consciously, deliberately attentive to this. Trusting for provisions when resources are widely scarce, handling the exhaustion of the situation, having some of the same questions about God and life that others may have, and the unrelenting ongoing challenges of combating temptations old and new, growing in personal sanctification,—all of these call for personal faithfulness to God. When people see your personal devotion to God as you are rejecting impatience, anger, fear, and doubt and instead are depending on God for personal finances, guidance and wisdom, physical strength, and the fruit of the Spirit—they know that you are not urging the same for them from a proverbial ivory tower. Your personal devotion to God can grant you authenticity.

Having an established consistent devotional life with Christ before a crisis provides a firm foundation from which to deal with the challenges of the crisis. With the time and energy demands of a NED, one must be intentional in maintaining this. Be realistic by accepting that one may not have hours to spend with God due to the emergency nature of some circumstances. But one can be daily consistent in allotting time with God in his Word and in prayer.

Be creative in the ways you maintain your faithfulness in devotional time. Touch base with God throughout the day. Prayer at mealtimes is not a ritual but an opportunity to consciously recognize God's goodness. If not able to actually be alone with God for personal devotions, invite those around you to join you in prayer or reading Scripture. Pastor Tom told me of playing worship music in the office of his secular work to provide something that encouraged his devotion.

Even as a preacher, one can likely experience faith challenges unrelated to doubting God's existence or one's own salvation. The great needs in a NED, the difficult circumstances, wrestling with suffering and natural evil as well as the choices of hard decisions may stretch one's faith and confidence in God's character. Stress, pressure, and fatigue will pose challenges to Christlikeness. All of these and more can be addressed by a vibrant devotional life.

A second priority for being faithful to God while living and preaching in the aftermath of an NED is *the integrity of God's character*. This intersects with being faithful in one's calling as it is true for the preacher's personal life as well as for preaching. Identify and share from the pulpit specific ongoing ways that God has shown his love and faithfulness both to you and to others during and in the aftermath of the NED. In the pulpit repeat often both the biblical examples and the local testimonies of God's character in the lives of people around you. Remind listeners that even in the most adverse circumstances such as in Joseph's life God still fulfilled his covenant with his people. Even if one chooses to see the NED as a divine message to the community, assure listeners—like Joel's preaching—that God is gracious, merciful, slow to anger, and abounding in steadfast love by calling for genuine repentance (Joel 2:13).

This priority of God's character should be maintained in your personal faith as well as in the pulpit. Remind yourself and those to whom you preach that God is unchangeable and is involved in the lives of his people even when one cannot see it at the moment. Contemplate how God is a faithful provider and encourage others to do the same. Publicly preach of God's goodness, kindness, and of his love for both his people and all of creation as is revealed in the Bible. You can draw from history and the current stories of local individuals that spotlight God's character. And . . . preach these truths to yourself!

Unfortunately, during the rebuilding phase of a NED opportunities abound to cut corners, fudge numbers and data, or exploit flaws in the system. Being a pastor or preacher does not make you immune to the temptations. And the financial pressure may become surprisingly heavy making the temptation to compromise even greater.

Being faithful to the character of God by being faithful in one's personal integrity does not need to be left unsaid. In Potiphar's house, Joseph was almost daily enticed by Potiphar's wife's sexual advances. His being faithful to God is what allowed God to bless him with the fullness of his covenant promises. In the short term, Joseph seemed to have paid a great price for his integrity. But in the long term that was not the case at all.

During recovery and rebuilding the temptations to compromise one's character promise quick returns but deliver long problems. Some municipalities affected by the Baton Rouge Flood of 2016 lost much potential help and aid from federal programs because of past mishandlings. But you being faithful to God's character in your personal integrity reaps something far more valuable than potential financial aid or gain—there is reputation, influence, spiritual power and authority, as well as the Lord's "Well, done" to be had.

The third priority is that of *humility both in the pulpit and toward people*. This is an often-forgotten act of faithfulness to God. Humility which accepts the limits of human ability directs attention to the limitlessness of God. The preacher that is humble before God is postured to actively listen to the stories of survivors, to be guarded with offering quick advice, to be appropriately transparent in the pulpit, and to avoid using harsh words or speaking with an abrasive tone. Humility is shown by a prayerful, habitual reliance on the Holy Spirit's empowering presence to enable and empower us to serve God's Word, his people, and the community. Humility also cautions us from confidently interpreting the event as divine judgment. And if as a preacher one does need to apply a biblical text as a call to evaluate one's personal life, doing so with humility makes the message more readily received by the listeners. They are hearing the message through someone who is not speaking as a demanding magistrate but as a humble messenger that cares for them.

The Levitical priests were given a special responsibility of ministering to the Lord as they carried the Ark of the Covenant in the wilderness and were called to bless his name. This special responsibility included ministering to the Lord, to attend to him as a worshipper (Deut 10:8). Your faithfulness to God in the aftermath of a NED is similar to ministering to the Lord.

Having as vibrant of a personal devotional life as possible ministers to him as you are placing a priority on the Lord's worth and glory. You are busy, tired, and likely frustrated. And seeing to it that time with God occurs in just such a season is a huge statement of how glorious he truly is. Your personal devotion proclaims to any who watch that God and time with him is a priority regardless.

And do not forget the intangible spiritual enrichment that comes through interacting with God in prayer and his Word. During a NED's aftermath people need to be around someone and talk with someone whose actions, attitudes, and words prompt peace, joy, wisdom, and even love. Being faithful to God in personal devotion is a fountainhead that overflows from your life into the lives of others.

CHAPTER TWENTY-ONE

The Situation Room

INSIDE THE WHITE HOUSE of Washington, DC, is a suite of rooms known by a singular designation—the Situation Room or Sit Room for short. During his term, President John F. Kennedy had become frustrated with the lag time of information that came to him about world situations. To address this, he created the communication center on the ground floor of the presidential residence. Then, as now, it is the nerve center for communication that the president needs in as near to real time as possible.

This room was a critical location September 11, 2001. It was on this date that the United States experienced the most orchestrated, wide-reaching terrorist attack in its history. As commercial airliners were hijacked and used as weapons against the United States, the entire world was thrown into confusion. Those in the Situation Room had been informed of a plane flying toward Washington, DC—the now infamous Flight 77. The entire Sit Room staff of around a dozen men and women were also told to evacuate along with the rest of all occupants of the White House to a predetermined safe location. It was suspected that the building was the intended target of the hijacked airplane. The response and actions of the Sit Room staff that day were publicly unknown for ten years.

When the call came that day to evacuate, senior duty officer Rob Hargis looked at the others around him and told them that they were being ordered to evacuate; if anyone wanted to leave, they were to do so now. As reported, the staff looked around at one another and without saying a word went back to their crucial duties of maintaining communication for the President of the United States during one of the greatest crises in American history. Hargis told the caller, "We are staying," and then went to the next call.

The calls that came in that day ranged from messages between frenetic American government agencies to highest level foreign government communications. As most any American citizen alive that day can say, the need for clear, reliable communication was critical. This need was not only for the President in making decisions but individual Americans and citizens of other nations in understanding and navigating how they were impacted by the events that day.[1]

Faithfulness. The men and women of the Situation Room in 2001 were faithful. Their faithfulness in their responsibilities, toward their duties, to their families, and to the nation was indubitably a key to the American government's ability to govern, guide, and simply speak to the world during the crisis.

Our role as preacher is similar to that of the staff of the Situation Room. We are the communication link through which passes God's message from his Word to his people and any others who will listen. Like the Situation Room staff, day-by-day, week-by-week we as preachers are called to and are measured by our faithfulness in the most ordinary of circumstances. But then there are those times when the importance and necessity of communication come to the forefront. And it is then that we must remain faithful regardless of the cost.

To those who have not experienced regular, long-term preaching responsibilities, I describe it as if one's soul is a sheet of paper. Each week and often more than once a week that sheet of paper is folded and creased then unfolded and flattened. It likely is not folded on the same line every time but wherever the folding and creasing occurs, it intersects with where it had been folded and creased before. And over time the constant folding, creasing, unfolding, and flattening begins to wear thin spots and eventually holes in the soul of a preacher. But the mercy of God, the grace of Christ, and the empowerment of the Holy Spirit renews the preacher's soul!

1. Duluth News Tribune, "As White House was evacuated, Duluth native stayed at his post on Sept. 11."

The Situation Room

The rhythm and repetition of preaching calls for one to be faithful. And, yes, being faithful with sermon preparation and delivery can wear one's soul. But during and after a natural environmental disaster, the preacher's degree of faithfulness is key to the situation. And the degree of the cost rises especially if the preacher has been personally affected by the disaster.

Preaching in a NED is similar to preaching at any other time. The preacher must prepare and deliver the sermon. For this task, the preacher uses both natural and learned skills surrendered to the empowering presence of the Holy Spirit. If you are the pastor of a local congregation you are preaching to many of the same people as you do each week.

However, preaching in a NED is also unlike preaching at other times. The listeners in this circumstance have experienced environmental trauma that has tremendously affected them physically, psychologically, socially, and spiritually. Their community and relationships have been dramatically, and likely unexpectedly, disrupted. They have experienced losses and are in some depth of grief. They are facing a process of recovery and rebuilding that, on the part of most of them, is a great unknown.

As the recovery and rebuild process unfolds, the listeners are growing more fatigued. They are experiencing multiple frustrations. Financial uncertainty nags at them. Governmental policies and decisions are affecting their lives in ways they never imagined. Relationships may be strained; unfortunately, some to a breaking point.

And on Sunday morning and maybe again that evening these people have chosen not to work on their homes, not to navigate paperwork and forms, not to leave town to get away from the pressure, and not to sleep in. They have chosen to come and hear a needed word from God. And the one that is expected to deliver this message has also experienced disruption, is facing the same unknowns, has also grown tired, is likely frustrated, has possibly struggled with relationships that week, and feels nagged by uncertainties. Yet that person is responsible to have studied, prepared, and now to stand to preach. That person is you!

While this book has drawn from published research on the subject, more importantly it has grown from the experiences of

SECTION FOUR

preachers that have served time in a Situation Room. They prepared and delivered sermons in a NED and have shared from their moment in disaster. As the next national or international crisis faced by a new staff of the Situation Room will be different than the one of September 11, 2001, so likely will yours be from these pastors. But their experiences and examples have something to offer for any future disaster you or others may face.

Daily, weekly, in rhythms and routines, but especially in the crisis of a natural environmental disaster–be faithful!

Bibliography

Advocate Staff Report. "What Caused the Historic August 2016 Flood, and What Are the Odds It Could Happen Again?" *The Advocate,* August 5, 2017. https://www.theadvocate.com/louisiana_flood_2016/article_3b7578fc-77b0-11e7-9aab-f7c07d05efcb.html.

American Psychiatric Association. *Diagnostic and Statistical Manual of Mental Disorders.* 5th ed. Arlington, VA: American Psychiatric Association, 2013.

———. "What is Posttraumatic Stress Disorder?" https://www.psychiatry.org/patients-families/ptsd/what-is-ptsd.

American Psychological Association. "Stress Effects on The Body." https://www.apa.org/topics/stress/body.

Anderson, Francis I. *Job: An Introduction and Commentary.* Tyndale Old Testament Commentaries 13, edited by D. J. Wisemen. Downers Grove: InterVarsity, 1976.

Aten, Jamie. "Preaching in the Wake of Disaster." *PreachingToday.* https://www.preachingtoday.com/skills/2016/july/preaching-in-wake-of-disaster.html.

Aten, J., and Boan D. Aten. *Spiritual First Aid: Disaster Chaplain Guide.* Wheaton, IL: Humanitarian Disaster Institute, Wheaton College, 2013.

Brueggeman, Walter. *Genesis: Interpretation A Bible Commentary for Teaching and Preaching.* Atlanta: John Knox, 1982.

Campbell, Robert Jean. *Psychiatric Dictionary.* New York: Oxford University Press, 1996.

Cherry, Katie E. *Lifespan Perspectives on Natural Disasters: Coping with Katrina, Rita, and Other Storms.* New York: Springer, 2009.

Clines, David J. A. *Job 1–20.* Word Biblical Commentary 17, edited by Bruce M. Metzger et al. Dallas: Word, 1989.

———. *Job 21–37.* Word Biblical Commentary 18A, edited by Bruce M. Metzger et al. Grand Rapids: Zondervan, 2006.

———. *Job 38–42.* Word Biblical Commentary 18B, edited by Bruce M. Metzger et al. Grand Rapids: Zondervan, 2011.

Bibliography

Di Liberto, Tom. "August 2016 Extreme Rain and Floods Along the Gulf Coast." *National Oceanic and Atmospheric Association.* https://www.climate.gov/news-features/event-tracker/august-2016-extreme-rain-and-floods-along-gulf-coast.

Duke, Anna, et al. "Natural Disasters as Moral Lessons: Nazianzus and New Orleans." *JSRNC* 6.1 (2012) 56–70.

"As White House Was Evacuated, Duluth Native Stays at His Post." *Duluth News Tribune,* September 11, 2011. https://www.duluthnewstribune.com/news/white-house-was-evacuated-duluth-native-stayed-his-post-sept-11.

Evans, Gary, ed. *Environmental Stress.* Cambridge: Cambridge University Press, 1982.

Fee, Gordon. *The First Epistle to the Corinthians.* Grand Rapids: Eerdmans, 1987.

Feimer, Nickolaus R., and Scott E. Geller, eds. *Environmental Psychology: Directions and Perspectives.* New York: Praeger, 1983.

Gauvin, Mary, et al. "Homes and Social Change: A Cross-Cultural Analysis." In *Environmental Psychology: Directions and Perspectives,* edited by Nickolaus R. Feimer and E. Scott Geller, 180–218. New York: Praeger, 1983.

Gist, Richard, and Bernard Lubin, eds. *Psychosocial Aspects of Disaster.* New York: Wiley, 1989.

Ghiloni, Aaron J., and Sylvie Shaw. "'Gumboot Religion': Religious Responses to an Australian Natural Disaster." *Journal for the Study of Religion, Nature, and Culture* 7.1 (2013) 27–48.

Gold, John R. *An Introduction to Behavioral Geography.* New York: Oxford, 1980.

Graham, Larry Kent. "Pastoral Theology and Catastrophic Disaster." *The Journal of Pastoral Theology* 16.1 (Fall 2006) 1–17.

Halpren, James and Mary Tramontin. *Disaster Mental Health: Theory and Practice.* Belmont, CA: Thomson, 2007.

Hubbard, David Allen. *Joel and Amos: An Introduction and Commentary.* Tyndale Old Testament Commentaries 25, edited by D. J. Wiseman. Downers Grove: InterVarsity, 1989.

Keller, Timothy. *Preaching: Communicating Faith in an Age of Skepticism.* New York: Viking, 2015.

Kidner, Derek. *Genesis: An Introduction and Commentary.* Tyndale Old Testament Commentaries 1, edited by D. J. Wiseman. Downers Grove: InterVarsity, 1967.

Kim, Matthew D. *Preaching with Cultural Intelligence: Understanding the People Who Hear Our Sermons.* Grand Rapids: Baker Academic, 2017.

Kuriansky, Judy. "Our Communities: Healing after Environmental Disasters." In *Living in an Environmentally Traumatized World: Healing Ourselves and Our Planet,* edited by Darlyne G. Nemeth et al., 141–68. Santa Barbara, CA: Praeger, 2012.

Lewis, Jack. *The Minor Prophets.* Grand Rapids, MI: Baker, 1966.

Lester, Andrew D. "Why Hast Thou Forsaken Me! Anger at God." *The Journal of Pastoral Theology* 16.1 (Fall 2006) 53–70.

Bibliography

Liftin, Duane. *Public Speaking: A Handbook for Christians*. 2nd ed. Grand Rapids: Baker, 1981.

National Weather Service. "Baton Rouge Ryan, LA. August 17, 2016". https://www.weather.gov/wrh/Climate?wfo=lix.

Nemeth, Darlyne Gaynor, Robert B. Hamilton, and Judith Kuriansky. *Ecopsychology: Advances from the Intersection of Psychology and Environmental Protection*. 2 vols. Santa Barbara, CA: Praeger, 2015.

Nemeth, Darlyne Gaynor, and Taighlor L. Whittington. "Our Human Resources: Coping with Environmental Changes." In *Living in an Environmentally Traumatized World: Healing Ourselves and Our Planet*, edited by Darlyne G. Nemeth et al., 113–40. Santa Barbara, CA: Praeger, 2012.

Nemeth, Darlyne Gaynor, and Traci W. Olivier. *Innovative Approaches to Individual and Community Resilience: From Theory to Practice*. London: Elsevier, 2017.

Ngwa, Kenneth. "Did Job Suffer for Nothing? The Ethics of Piety, Presumption and the Reception of Disaster in the Prologue of Job." *Journal for the Study of the Old Testament* 33.3 (2009) 359–80.

Oswalt, John N. "Barak." In *Theological Wordbook of the Old Testament*, edited by R. Laird Harris et al., 1:132–33. Chicago: Moody, 1980.

Reed, John P. "The Pastoral Care of Victims of Major Disasters." *The Journal of Pastoral Care* 31.2 (June 1977) 97–108.

Rentfrow, Peter, ed. *Geographical Psychology: Exploring the Interaction of Environment and Behavior*. Washington, DC: American Psychological Association, 2014.

Rezaeian, Mohsen. "The Adverse Psychological Outcomes of Natural Disasters: How Religion May Help to Disrupt the Connection." *The Journal of Pastoral Care and Counseling* 62.3 (Fall 2008) 289–92.

Shumaker, Sally Ann, and Ralph B. Taylor. "Toward a Clarification of People-Place Relationships: A Model of Attachment to Place." In *Environmental Psychology: Directions and Perspectives*, edited by Nickolaus R. Feimer and E. Scott Geller, 219–51. New York: Praeger, 1983.

Stott, John. *Between Two Worlds: The Challenge of Preaching Today*. Grand Rapids: Eerdmans, 1982.

Stuart, Douglas. *Hosea-Jonah*. Word Biblical Commentary 31, edited by David A. Hubbard and Glenn W. Barker. Waco, TX: Word, 1987.

Taylor, A. J. W. *Disasters and Disaster Stress: Stress in Modern Society 10*. New York: AMS, 1989.

Tierney, Kathleen J. "The Social and Community Contexts of Disaster," in *Psychosocial Aspects of Disaster*, edited by Richard Gist and Bernard Lubin, 11–39. New York: Wiley and Sons, 1989.

Tsevat, Matitiahu. "The Meaning of the Book of Job." *Hebrew Union College Annual* 37 (1966) 73–106.

Wapner, Seymour, et al., eds. *Experiencing the Environment*. New York: Plenum, 1976.

Bibliography

Wenham, Gordon J. *Genesis 1–15*. Word Biblical Commentary, edited by David A. Hubbard. Waco, TX: Word, 1987.

Winter, Bruce W. "Secular and Christian Responses to Corinthian Famines." *Tyndale Bulletin* 40 (1989) 86–106.

World Health Organization. "Burden of Mental and Behavioral Disorders." In *The World Health Report of 2001 Mental Health: New Understanding, New Hope*, 44. Geneva, Switzerland: World Health Organization, 2001.

Zelinski, Susan. "Our Critical Issues in Coping with Environmental Changes: The Intersection of Nature, Psychology, and Spirituality." In *Living in an Environmentally Traumatized World: Healing Ourselves and Our Planet*, edited by Darlyne G. Nemeth, Robert Hamilton, Judy Kuriansky, 169–78. Santa Barbara, CA: Praeger, 2012.

www.ingramcontent.com/pod-product-compliance
Lightning Source LLC
Chambersburg PA
CBHW072150160426
43197CB00012B/2324